Contents

Preparing to Write

Functions

Cohesion

Clarity, Style and Tone

Structure

Punctuation

British and American Spellings

Common Problems

Sample Business Letters

Use of symbols in this book

This warning symbol indicates common problems and important points.

This indicates additional information worth noting.

This refers to other chapters or sections with relevant information.

These flags show the differences between British and American English.

Preparing to Write

Introduction

Writing a business letter or report in a foreign language is not easy. Writing follows thinking and people usually think in their first language.

Careful preparation is needed to write well. You should ask yourself a number of important questions before you start. The answers to these questions will help you to plan what you are going to write and will help you to write more effectively.

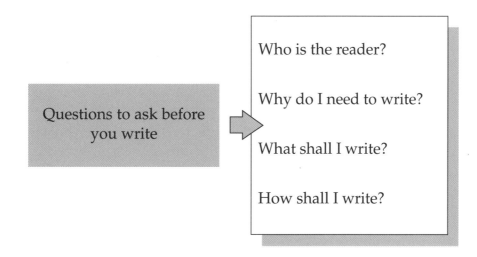

Questions to ask before you write

Who is the reader?

Why do I need to write?

What shall I write?

How shall I write?

2 Who is the reader?

The first important question to ask yourself is '**Who is the reader?**'. The answer to this question will affect how and what you write.

Experts and jargon

Many business letters, reports and memos* are written by experts, specialists in certain areas of business. However, the person who will read the letter, report or memo is very often not an expert in that area. For example, you may be a lawyer, a tax adviser, a financial expert or a computer specialist, writing a letter to a non-specialist client.

Every specialised subject has very specific and often technical language which is unfamiliar to non-specialists. It is therefore very important:

- not to use too much technical jargon
- to paraphrase when necessary, in other words, try to explain technical items in simpler language
- to have very clear explanations for anything that the reader may find difficult to understand

* 'Memoranda' is the plural form of the word; the singular form is 'memorandum'. Often, the shortened form is used: 'memos' and 'memo' respectively.

Exclude non-essential information

You also need to think about what the reader needs to know. Cut down on everything but the essential information. You will not want to tell the reader what he or she already knows although you may wish to refer to shared information. If you are giving the reader information that is completely new, you will have to state this information very clearly.

The reader's attitude

It may also be helpful to consider the reader's attitude.

- Is the reader likely to be interested in what you are writing? If not, you should think about what you can do to stimulate the reader's interest.
- If you are writing something which may annoy the reader, it may be important to use tactful language.

Formality

How well you know the reader is also important. Is your letter, report or memo for internal communication within your own company, or is it for external communication with another company, or to a customer or client? If you have never met the reader(s), your letter is likely to be more formal in style than it would be if you know them quite well. Reports are always written in a formal style.

Summary

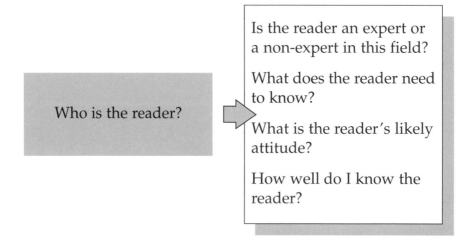

Who is the reader?

Is the reader an expert or a non-expert in this field?

What does the reader need to know?

What is the reader's likely attitude?

How well do I know the reader?

Why do I need to write?

The second important question is 'Why do I need to write?'. Writing is not the only form of communication. Is it absolutely essential to write when you could, for example, make a telephone call instead? A telephone call will be much quicker.

Writing is essential however:

- when you need a record, perhaps for legal purposes
- when you have to convey complicated information
- when you have been asked to prepare a report or submit a proposal

This will give the reader time to think and to respond to what you have written. You may need to write to confirm arrangements made by telephone, for example, to confirm the date and time of a meeting, or the details of an order.

Aims and objectives

It is important to establish the aims and objectives of your writing. Business people write for many different reasons:

- you may be acting as an adviser, reporting on your investigations into a particular subject and making recommendations
- you may be writing a proposal to your colleagues or superiors, for example, a capital expenditure proposal

- you may be writing to persuade customers to buy something
- you may be writing a letter to order something or to complain or apologise

Recognising your objective at the beginning helps you to focus clearly on the information you need to communicate and the way in which to do it. It will help you to choose the kind of language to use and the style in which to write. It will also help you to select the relevant information and to organise it in such a way that you achieve your aims.

Summary

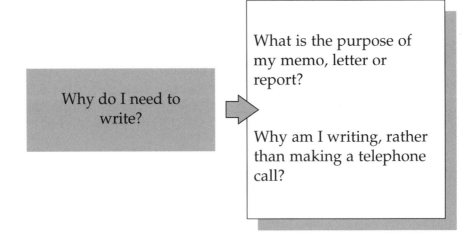

Why do I need to write?

What is the purpose of my memo, letter or report?

Why am I writing, rather than making a telephone call?

4 What shall I write?

Another important question is '**What shall I write?**'. The answer to this question could be either the form of the writing or the content itself.

Form

Writing can take the form of a letter, a report, or a memo. These can be typed (word processed), or produced by a desktop publishing system. Sometimes, it is useful to write a short letter or memo by hand. Your letter, report or memo can be sent by post, by fax or electronically, by e-mail.

- Letters to external organisations present an image of the company and so they need to be clearly set out according to certain conventions. Letters written in English follow a very specific layout, different from that in many other European countries.

- A report usually follows a conventional format. Reports are largely factual and targeted at a specific audience.

- A memo (or inter-office communication) is normally to colleagues within a company and is shorter and less formal than a business letter.

- A fax message usually reaches the recipient immediately and you can receive an immediate answer. A fax is, however, essentially a public document and so you should not include anything confidential in it.

- An e-mail (electronic mail) message is a computerised method of exchanging information, often used for both internal and external communication.

Content

After establishing your goals, you will need to collect all the necessary information and to focus on what is essential for the reader to know. The next step is planning the writing, organising and sorting the information into a clear and logical format. A sensible way of dealing with this is to write down all the main points and then try to organise them into a logical sequence.

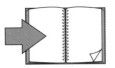

See Chapters 52-55.

Summary

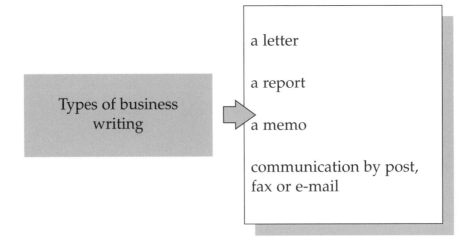

Types of business writing

a letter

a report

a memo

communication by post, fax or e-mail

How shall I write?

The last important question to ask yourself is '**How shall I write?**'. This question is about the type of language to use and how to organise it.

Language

You will need to choose the correct vocabulary, grammar and functional language to use. Your choice of language affects the understanding of the reader. If you use a functional phrase such as 'May we draw your attention to...', it is obvious that you are then going to write something that is very important for the reader. If you write 'We recommend that...', it is clear that you are about to make a recommendation. These phrases act as helpful signals to the reader.

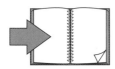

See sections on *Functions* (Chapters 7-28) and *Common Problems* (Chapters 67-69).

Clarity, style and tone

Clarity is affected by the length of your sentences and the grammatical structures that you use. In general, short sentences using simple constructions are clearer than long, complicated ones. Style is also very important. You will need to consider how you can vary your sentences and how formal your language should be. You will also need to think about tone (how strongly you wish to phrase a recommendation, for example).

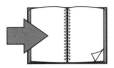

See section on *Clarity, Style and Tone* (Chapters 47-50).

Using paragraphs

The language you use needs to be well-organised so that it is easy to read. This means dividing it up logically into paragraphs (with headings and sub-headings in longer letters and reports). Each paragraph needs to be linked to the next one.

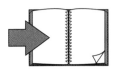

See section on *Structure* (Chapters 51-59).

Cohesion

The text itself needs to be cohesive, which means that the words, sentences and ideas need to be joined together, avoiding repetition where possible.

See section on *Cohesion* (Chapters 29-46).

Summary

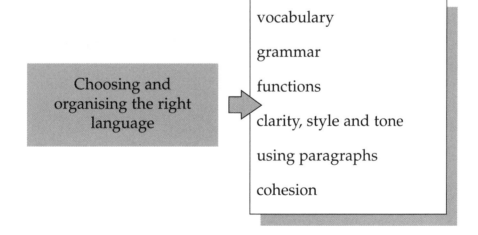

Writing process

Finally, having answered all the **Who?**, **Why?**, **What?** and **How?** questions, you are ready to begin writing.

When you are writing a complex letter or report, it is advisable to write a draft first. This is a 'rough' copy which you will then evaluate and review where necessary. Check that your language is correct and that your message is clear and logically presented. Always look at your writing from the reader's point of view. Considering the reader is the most important aspect of the writing process.

A summary of the writing process is shown on the opposite page.

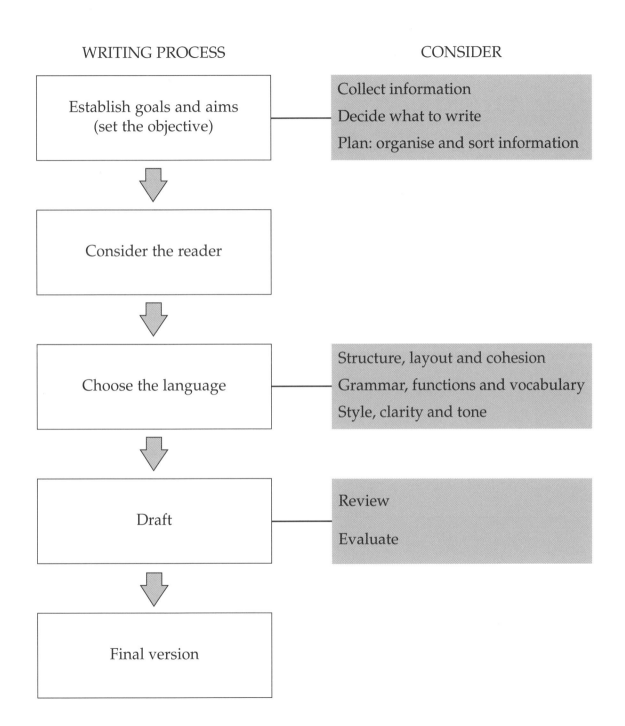

WRITING PROCESS   CONSIDER

| Establish goals and aims (set the objective) | Collect information
Decide what to write
Plan: organise and sort information |

Consider the reader

| Choose the language | Structure, layout and cohesion
Grammar, functions and vocabulary
Style, clarity and tone |

| Draft | Review
Evaluate |

Final version

Functions

Introduction

7

This section of the book:

- looks at different functions used in writing
- shows words and phrases that are used for each function.

What are functions?

We use language, both spoken and written, for particular purposes. Functions are the purposes for which people speak or write. You may want to:

- give advice or make a recommendation
- give an example
- explain something
- show that one thing is the result or consequence of another.

These are examples of functions. There are special words and phrases that people use to express functions. These words and phrases act as **signals** to the reader, for example,

> **We would recommend that you** postpone the meeting until the following week.

It is clear to the reader that this is a recommendation.

When you write letters or reports, you may need to:

- express certainty, probability, possibility or doubt
- contrast between two or more facts, choices or options
- emphasise how important something is
- explain something
- express alternatives
- focus the reader's attention
- generalise
- give examples
- give opinions, suggestions, advice and recommendations
- make reference
- say what method is used to do something
- express obligation or necessity
- offer further assistance
- use polite phrases
- express purpose
- give results and consequences
- give sequences or lists
- state conclusions
- state conditions
- state understanding or assumptions
- summarise

Functional phrases in letters

make reference	**With reference to your letter of** 28 February regarding the possible purchase of software for your accounting systems,
polite phrases	**we have pleasure in** enclosing details of our spreadsheet programmes.
recommendation	**We would recommend that** you consider purchasing the 2XZ package which seems to be the most suitable for your purposes.
focus attention	**May we draw your attention to** the fact that there is a special discount on this product during March.
offer of further assistance	**If you have any further questions, please do not hesitate to contact us.**
polite ending	**We look forward to hearing from you.**

Dear Mr. Johnson,

With reference to your letter of 28 February regarding the possible purchase of software for your accounting systems, **we have pleasure in** enclosing details of our spreadsheet programmes.

We would recommend that you consider purchasing the 2XZ package which seems to be the most suitable for your purposes.

May we draw your attention to the fact that there is a special discount on this product during March.

If you have any further questions, please do not hesitate to contact us.

We look forward to hearing from you.

Yours sincerely,

James Benson
Regional Sales Manager

Making reference

8

At the beginning of a letter or report, a writer often refers to:

- an earlier letter or report
- a previous meeting or telephone conversation
- a request from the reader

Referring to an earlier letter or conversation

Thank you for	your letter of 26 October.
	your recent letter, ref PR104.

With reference to	your letter of 26 October,...
I/We refer to	our recent telephone conversation,...
Further to	our meeting on 16 February,...

Referring to a request

As requested,	I am enclosing a copy of our current brochure.

Referring to a published document

In the middle of a letter or report, a writer sometimes refers to a published document.

I/We refer you to I/We would refer you to	clause 25 of your lease contract which states that...

Polite phrases

9

Polite phrases are often used at the beginning and end of a business letter. They can be used when:

- sending (enclosing) something with a letter or
- referring to the reader's future reply or to a meeting with the reader.

Enclosing something with a letter

We are pleased to	send you a copy of our brochure.
	submit our invoice in connection with recent consultancy services.

We have pleasure in	sending you a copy of our brochure.
	submitting our invoice in connection with recent consultancy services.

Please find enclosed	a copy of our brochure.
	our invoice in connection with recent consultancy services.

Referring to a future reply or to a meeting

I/We look forward to	meeting you on 5 July.
	hearing from you.
	your early reply.

10 Stating understanding

A writer sometimes:

- tells the reader that the facts about to be mentioned are believed to be correct or that they are understood to be correct from what the writer has already been told
- explains the assumption on which the writer has based an opinion, forecast, or recommendation

Stating understanding

I/We understand that **I/We believe that**	you are a supplier of Power Mac computers.

It is our understanding that	you do not wish to accept the proposed contract terms.

Stating assumptions

The estimated cost of the interest on the bank loan will be $100,000 over two years,	**assuming**	an interest rate of 8%.

On the assumption that	the weather stays fine, we expect the construction work to be completed on time.

It is assumed that **We assume that**	Mr Smith will be resident here in 2000.

Generalising

A writer may wish to point out the general rules or normal conditions that apply in a situation.

As a general rule, **As a rule,**	the managers we appoint to run our subsidiaries in each country must be local nationals.

In general, **Generally,** **Normally,**	employees work a minimum of thirty-six hours a week.

On the whole,	we are very satisfied with the quality of the materials you supply and the promptness of your deliveries.

Explaining

When a writer has made a point or used a word that may be difficult for the reader to understand, he or she may explain or define the meaning in other words.

Each highly paid employee,	**in other words,**	each employee earning more than $100,000 a year, will be invited to join the incentive scheme.

Each highly paid employee,	**i.e.**	each employee earning more than $100,000 a year, will be invited to join the incentive scheme.

All residents, except temporary residents, will be subject to taxation.	**This means that**	all residents who stay in the country for longer than six months will be taxed.

i.e. = 'id est' (Latin meaning 'that is')

13 Giving opinions and recommendations

In many letters and reports, a writer gives:

- **an opinion**. The opinion or belief may be strongly held, but the writer does not suggest any action.
- **a suggestion**. This is something the writer thinks the reader might like to consider, but it is not a particularly strong piece of advice.
- **advice** and **recommendations** which are given on the basis of knowledge or expertise. There is very little difference between advice and recommendation. It is often a matter of strength or tone.

Opinion

In my/our view, **In my/our opinion,** **I am/We are (strongly) of the opinion that**	the increase in salaries last year was too high and more than the company can afford to pay.

Suggestions

I/We suggest that We would suggest that It is suggested that	you arrange a meeting to discuss ways of preventing late deliveries in the future.

Advice

I/We would (strongly) advise you to It is advisable to	fly to Riga via Stockholm. It is quicker than going via Copenhagen.

You might like to consider	flying to Riga via Stockholm. It is quicker than going via Copenhagen.

You should It is in your interest to	visit Mr Ortega when you are in Pamplona.

Recommendations

I/We (strongly) recommend that It is recommended that	the new office be located in Vienna.

It is essential that It is of the utmost importance that	you improve the safety procedures immediately.

Strength of advice and recommendations

It is necessary for the reader to understand the degree of importance given to advice and recommendations by the writer. Sometimes, the writer gives a piece of advice that the reader can choose to act on or to ignore as he or she wishes. Sometimes, it may be very important or legally necessary for the reader to carry out the action.

See Chapter 50, *Tone*.

Strength of advice and recommendations

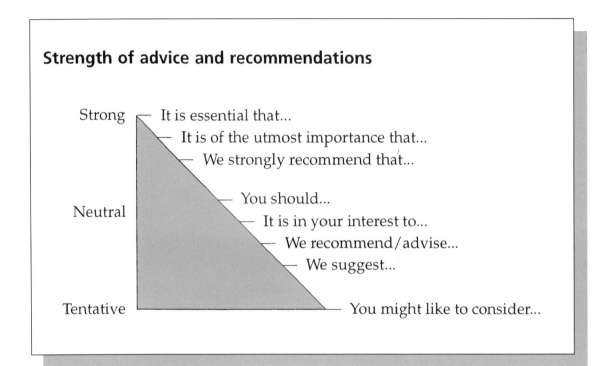

Strong — It is essential that...
— It is of the utmost importance that...
— We strongly recommend that...

Neutral — You should...
— It is in your interest to...
— We recommend/advise...
— We suggest...

Tentative — You might like to consider...

Expressing obligation/necessity

14

Sometimes a writer has to inform the reader that there is a necessity or legal obligation to carry out certain actions.

It is	obligatory compulsory	to register the new company within 30 days.

The Ministry of Commerce	is obliged (by law) is required	to respond within three months to your request.

A claims form	must has to	be submitted as soon as possible.

You	**must** / **are required to**	submit a monthly report to Head Office.

It is essential that	you notify the authorities about this decision immediately.

Expressing degrees of certainty

15

A writer sometimes wishes to express how certain something is.

Certainty

It is certain that	
There is no doubt that	the cause of the accident was a fault in the engine.
I am certain that	
We are confident that	

Probability

It is probable that	we shall exceed our sales target for the year.
It is likely that	

Possibility

Local taxes	**can** **may**	sometimes be lower in development zones.

The strike	**could**	last for several weeks.

A change in government	**might (possibly)**	force us to reconsider our investment decision.

Doubt

It is doubtful whether **There is some doubt as to whether**	Mr Schmidt will be able to attend the meeting.

I doubt whether	they will agree to these conditions.

Improbability

The reduction in interest rates is	unlikely	to affect consumer spending for at least six months.

Impossibility

Early delivery of the goods is	impossible	at such short notice.

Degrees of certainty

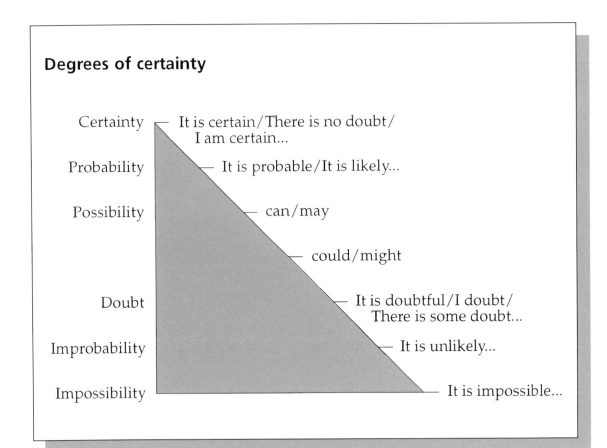

Certainty	It is certain/There is no doubt/ I am certain...
Probability	It is probable/It is likely...
Possibility	can/may
	could/might
Doubt	It is doubtful/I doubt/ There is some doubt...
Improbability	It is unlikely...
Impossibility	It is impossible...

Focusing attention

16

A writer focuses the reader's attention on something when he or she wants the reader to be aware of something or to note something.

I should like to draw your attention to **May I/we draw your attention to**	Clause 12 of the (enclosed) contract which has been amended.

We would like to point out that **It should be noted that** **Please note that**	the listed prices do not include Value Added Tax.

Contrasting

17

A writer sometimes refers to two facts or options and makes a contrast between them. Quite often, when making a contrast, the less important fact or less attractive option is mentioned first.

In spite of Despite	poor short-term forecasts,	we expect positive results in the long-term.

In spite of the fact that Despite the fact that	a resident company is entitled to deduct 20% from dividends,	this seldom happens.

Whereas While Although Even though	the level of processing errors has been reduced,	it is still far too high.

The services provided by the software company are very expensive.	However,	the company has a first-class reputation for quality.

The Japanese suppliers have put forward a very interesting proposal.	On the other hand,	having a supplier in Europe would be much more practical.

Emphasising

18

Sometimes, a writer needs to indicate that something is either:

- important
- very important

Emphasising that something is important

I/We would like to remind you that It is important to remember that	payment is due by 31 March.

It must be remembered that It is worth noting/remembering that	this is only a preliminary review.

Emphasising that something is very important

It is of the utmost importance that	we should expand our operations into South-East Asia.

I should like to stress	the importance of expanding our operations into South-East Asia.

This issue is	of the utmost importance. crucial. vital.

This report is highly confidential.	On no account Under no circumstances	should you discuss it with anyone else.

19 Expressing alternatives

Often, a writer wishes to inform the reader that there is more than one possible choice or course of action.

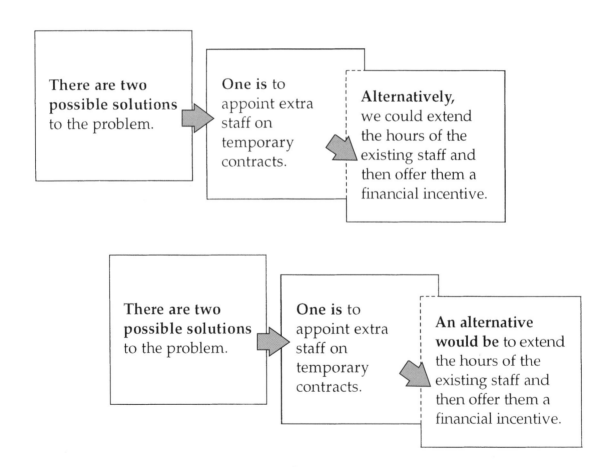

There are two **possible solutions** to the problem.

One is to appoint extra staff on temporary contracts.

Alternatively, we could extend the hours of the existing staff and then offer them a financial incentive.

There are two **possible solutions** to the problem.

One is to appoint extra staff on temporary contracts.

An alternative would be to extend the hours of the existing staff and then offer them a financial incentive.

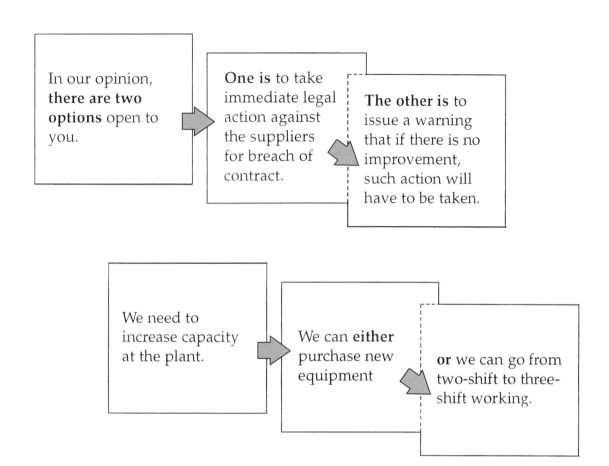

In our opinion, **there are two options** open to you.

One is to take immediate legal action against the suppliers for breach of contract.

The other is to issue a warning that if there is no improvement, such action will have to be taken.

We need to increase capacity at the plant.

We can **either** purchase new equipment

or we can go from two-shift to three-shift working.

Giving examples

20

Writers often give examples of a point just mentioned.

Security procedures in the buildings have been improved.	**For example,** **For instance,** **To give an example,**	staff must now carry an identity card at all times.

Many banks lost money on bad loans to customers.	**A case in point is**	X Bank whose profits fell by over $1 billion last year because of bad debts.

Other factors,	**such as**	the attitude of employees, should be considered before we reach a decision.

The company is suffering from a severe shortage of skills,	**e.g.**	in engineering design and information technology skills. We need to improve our recruitment and training policy.

Be careful about the different uses of '**e.g.**' and '**i.e.**'.

    e.g. (Latin 'exempli gratia') = for example

    i.e. (Latin 'id est')   = that is (used for an explanation)

Both these shortened forms are used in informal letters, memos and faxes, but not in formal letters.

21 Offering further assistance

At the end of a letter, the writer sometimes offers further assistance or to supply further information should the reader need it.

If you have any further questions,	**we shall be happy to answer them.**
Should you have any further questions,	

Should you require any further information,	**please do not hesitate to contact us.**

Please do not hesitate to contact us	should you require any further information.

Please let me know if I can be of further assistance.*

* informal

22 Sequencing and listing

A writer frequently needs to give:

- a **sequence** of actions to be carried out or that have been carried out. At the beginning of a complex letter or report, they may also wish to show how they will sequence the different points they wish to make
- a **list** of related facts

Sequencing

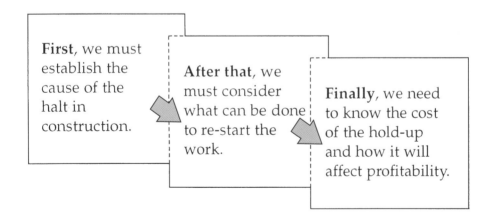

First, we must establish the cause of the halt in construction.

After that, we must consider what can be done to re-start the work.

Finally, we need to know the cost of the hold-up and how it will affect profitability.

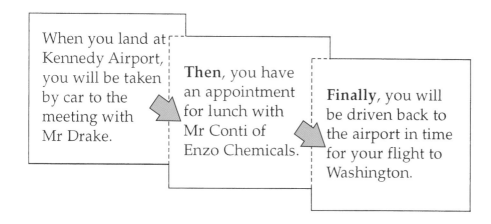

When you land at Kennedy Airport, you will be taken by car to the meeting with Mr Drake.

Then, you have an appointment for lunch with Mr Conti of Enzo Chemicals.

Finally, you will be driven back to the airport in time for your flight to Washington.

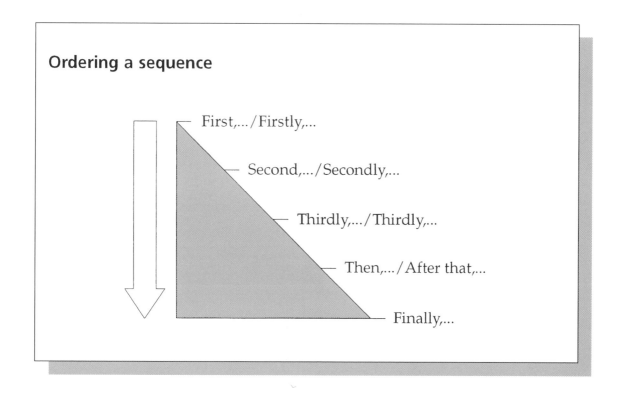

Ordering a sequence

First,.../Firstly,...

Second,.../Secondly,...

Thirdly,.../Thirdly,...

Then,.../After that,...

Finally,...

Listing

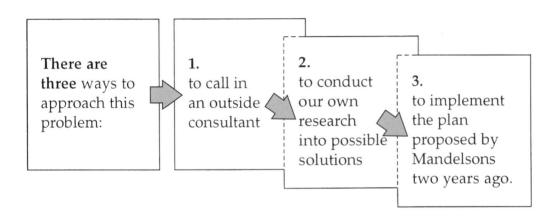

There are **three** ways to approach this problem:

1. to call in an outside consultant

2. to conduct our own research into possible solutions

3. to implement the plan proposed by Mandelsons two years ago.

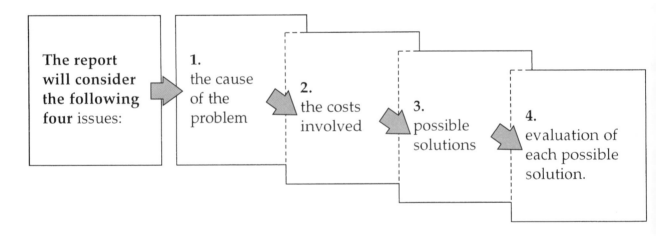

The report **will consider the following four** issues:

1. the cause of the problem

2. the costs involved

3. possible solutions

4. evaluation of each possible solution.

23 Stating results and consequences

When certain actions are taken, there are often results or consequences which the writer wishes to mention.

We were unsure about the correct procedures to take,	**so** we asked Head Office for guidance.

We were unsure about the correct procedures, we	**therefore** asked Head Office for guidance.

Our decision to close the factory is a	**consequence** of the removal of government subsidies for new investments in the region.

The law on fringe benefits has changed. We will	**consequently** have to review the tax positions of your staff.

Reduce the number of workers in a company and the	**result** is lower running costs.

As a result of the recent sales drive, **As a consequence** of the recent sales drive,	our turnover has increased substantially.

Stating purpose

A writer may wish to indicate that an action is carried out to achieve an objective or purpose.

The company has decided to reduce the number of workers by 10% over the next two years	**in order to** reduce running costs.

Staff training must be completed by the end of the month	**so that** the timetable for introducing the new system can be met.

I should be grateful if we could postpone the meeting until the following week	**to** give me time to study the report.

Stating method

25

A writer may want to indicate how something can be achieved (the method for achieving it).

Profits can be increased	**by raising** our selling prices.

The project was completed on time	**by** employing extra workers.

Errors can be avoided	**by** careful attention to detail.

Time can be saved	**by** using freelance workers.

Remember that **verbs** immediately following prepositions end in '...**ing**' ('by rais**ing**', 'by employ**ing**', etc.).

Stating conditions

26

A writer often has to inform the reader that certain conditions have to be fulfilled before an action can be taken or before a fact becomes true. In written English, there are three types of condition that are often used in business letters and reports. They are:

- about general truths, laws, or rules, providing a certain condition is met. (**Conditional 0**)
- about a future result that may or will occur if a certain condition is fulfilled. (The fulfilling of the condition is thought to be a real possibility.) (**Conditional 1**)
- about a result that would occur if a certain condition were fulfilled. (The fulfilling of the condition is less likely and more hypothetical.) (**Conditional 2**)

General truths, laws, and rules (Conditional 0)

RESULT	CONDITION
Customers **are permitted** to make copies of our software	if they **have** a licensing agreement.

CONDITION	RESULT
If you **are** a citizen of an EU country,	you **can work** in any other country in the European Union.

CONDITION	RESULT
If more than 50% of the shares of Company A **are owned** by Company B,	Company A **is regarded** as a subsidiary of Company B.

CONDITION	RESULT
Unless you **are** qualified,	you **are not permitted** to sell insurance to the general public.

Real possibilities (Conditional 1)

CONDITION	RESULT
If trading conditions **deteriorate,**	we **will revise** our financial forecasts.

RESULT	CONDITION
The factory **will be closed down**	**unless** it **receives** a major new order.

Hypothetical or unlikely situations (Conditional 2)

CONDITION	RESULT
If we **were to relocate** to the Republic of Ireland,	our tax position **would change** radically.

CONDITION	RESULT
If you **restructured** the company,	you **could reduce** costs.

Conditional 2 is often used for a 'tentative suggestion':

If you **opened** a branch in Sweden, you **would** be able to sell into Finland and Norway too.

The company may not have discussed the possibility seriously yet. The meaning is:

Let's consider what would happen if you opened a branch in Sweden.

A change to **Conditional 1** indicates a 'stronger possibility' that the condition will be fulfilled.

If you **open** a branch in Sweden, you **will** be able to sell into Finland and Norway too.

In this case, the company is already considering taking this action – there is a real possibility that they will open a branch in Sweden.

Stating conclusions

27

After giving the background facts of a situation or problem and the possible courses of action, a writer often states the conclusion he or she has reached. A conclusion is not a recommendation; it is the writer's interpretation of the situation or problem as he or she understands it.

CONCLUSION

We conclude, therefore,	that TV advertising has been the most cost-effective type of advertising for the company in the last five years.

CONCLUSION

From our findings, **we have reached the conclusion that**	if this course of action is taken, existing clients will be lost.

It is concluded that	there are enormous differences in trading conditions in these two areas.

Summarising

28

At the end of a complex letter or report, a writer usually gives a brief summary.

SUMMARY

To sum up,	the implications of this action would be: 1. the reduction of production in the northern region 2. the increase of production in the southern region.

SUMMARY

To summarise,	we would recommend further research into the market potential in South-East Asia.

Briefly then,*	the implications are as follows: 1. the employees' housing allowances would cost the company £250,000 2. the employees would be taxed on this allowance.

* informal

Cohesion

What is cohesion?

29

Cohesion means 'holding together', or 'linking'.

Words, sentences, paragraphs and ideas in letters, reports and memos are linked together by:

- connectors
- reference words
- referring to other parts of a text

Connectors

Connectors are joining words and phrases, for example, '**although**' and '**in spite of**'. They are used to link two ideas. They can also be used to give a signal to the reader of a function like '**contrasting**', for example:

Although the company was established just two years ago, it is already renowned for the quality of its products.

Reference words

Reference words, eg. '**who**', '**which**', '**this**' are used to refer to people, things, and ideas that have already been mentioned in the letter or report. The writer wishes to mention these topics again and by using reference words, he or she avoids repeating other words. For example:

> The company relocated to the north of England last year. **This** resulted in considerable financial savings.

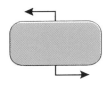

Referring to other parts of a text

To make a complex or lengthy text more comprehensible to a reader, it is also important for the writer to **refer to other parts of the text**, for example, an earlier or later part, or to refer to a visual. Reference to other parts of the text can be made by using expressions such as '**as follows**', '**see above**', '**the graph below**', etc.

Cohesion in letters and reports

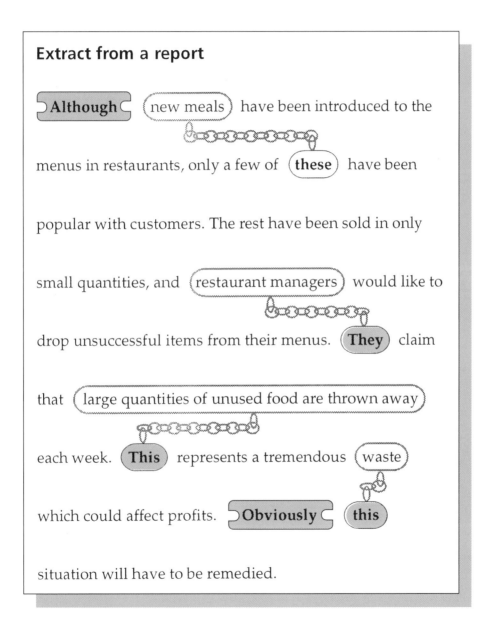

Extract from a report

Although (new meals) have been introduced to the menus in restaurants, only a few of (**these**) have been popular with customers. The rest have been sold in only small quantities, and (restaurant managers) would like to drop unsuccessful items from their menus. (**They**) claim that (large quantities of unused food are thrown away) each week. (**This**) represents a tremendous (waste) which could affect profits. **Obviously** (**this**) situation will have to be remedied.

Connectors: Introduction

30

Connectors:

- join one idea or statement to another
- indicate to the reader how or why statements are connected (that is, they signal which function is being used)

Connectors are used for:

- adding relevant points
- comparing and contrasting
- conditions
- giving reasons
- highlighting

31 Connectors: Adding relevant points

We use some connectors to make additional points (to introduce an idea or statement that adds to something that has already been written).

This year, we expect to recruit thirty graduates with business degrees to work in the administration and finance departments. **In addition,** we shall recruit another twenty graduates with engineering degrees.

The company has expanded, **not only** in its home market, **but also** in markets throughout Europe and Asia.

As well as | providing our customers with a quality sales service, | we also offer an excellent returns policy.

We are planning to set up agencies in Japan and | furthermore, | we may consider going into China at a later stage.

32 Connectors: Comparisons/contrasts

Connectors can be used to compare or contrast two things or ideas as follows:

- comparing or contrasting relative size, rate or amount
- contrasting between positive and negative qualities (e.g. advantages and disadvantages)
- contrasting between two different situations

Comparing or contrasting relative size, rate or amount

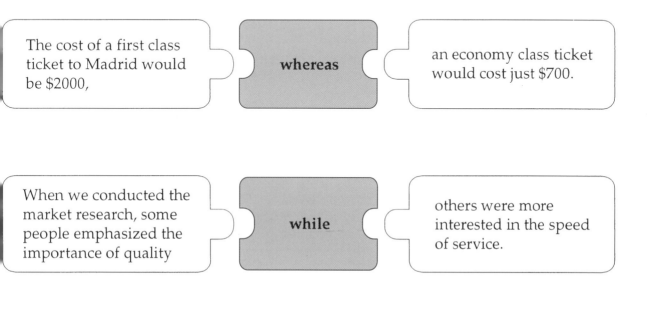

The cost of a first class ticket to Madrid would be $2000, **whereas** an economy class ticket would cost just $700.

When we conducted the market research, some people emphasized the importance of quality **while** others were more interested in the speed of service.

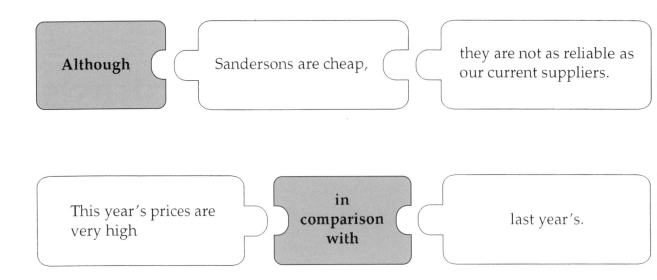

| Although | Sandersons are cheap, | they are not as reliable as our current suppliers. |

| This year's prices are very high | in comparison with | last year's. |

Contrasting between positive and negative qualities

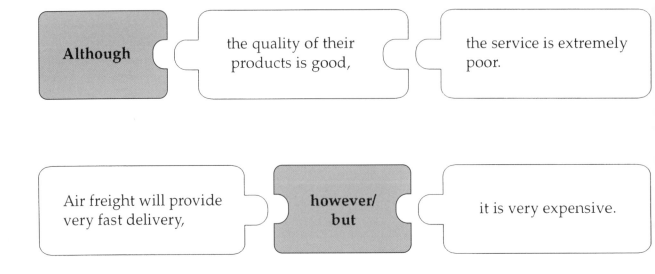

| Although | the quality of their products is good, | the service is extremely poor. |

| Air freight will provide very fast delivery, | however/ but | it is very expensive. |

Contrasting between two different situations, ideas or possibilities

The report has not yet been received,	despite the fact that	we asked for it three weeks ago.

I believe that the new product will be successful,	even though	the competition is strong.

We were unable to complete the work on time last month,	in spite of	our staff working overtime.

You could relocate to the North of England.	Alternatively,	you could use the site of the former plant, situated near the docks.

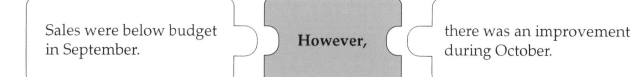

Sales were below budget in September. | However, | there was an improvement during October.

'In spite of' and 'despite' can be followed either by a verb in the '...ing' form or by 'the fact that':

In spite of/Despite employing extra staff, we found it difficult to complete the job on time.

In spite of the fact that/Despite the fact that we employed extra staff, we found it difficult to complete the job on time.

33 Connectors: In conditional sentences

Connectors can be used in sentences which state conditions.

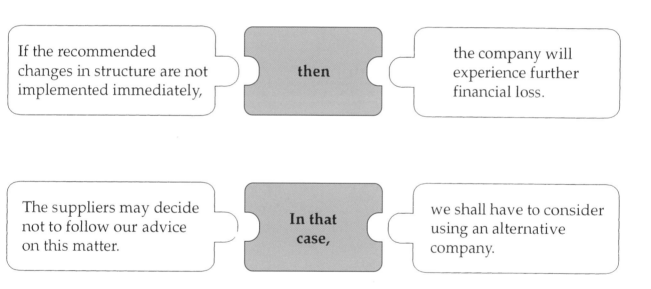

| If the recommended changes in structure are not implemented immediately, | **then** | the company will experience further financial loss. |

| The suppliers may decide not to follow our advice on this matter. | **In that case,** | we shall have to consider using an alternative company. |

See Chapter 26, *Stating Conditions*.

34 Connectors: Giving reasons

We can use connectors to give reasons for:

- situations or actions
- courses of action that you are recommending

Reasons for situations or actions

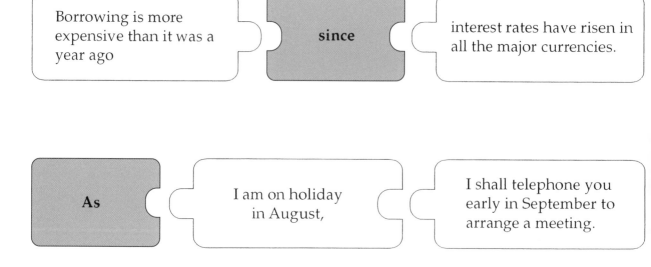

Borrowing is more expensive than it was a year ago **since** interest rates have risen in all the major currencies.

As I am on holiday in August, I shall telephone you early in September to arrange a meeting.

Reasons for recommended courses of action

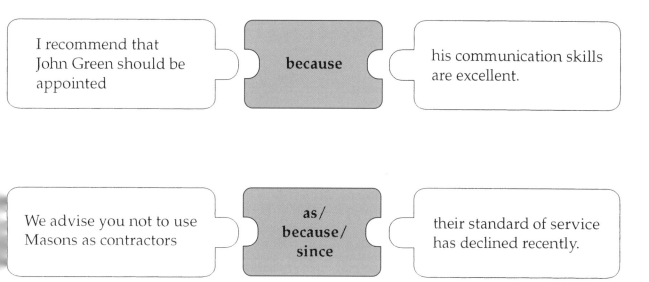

I recommend that John Green should be appointed	**because**	his communication skills are excellent.
We advise you not to use Masons as contractors	**as/ because/ since**	their standard of service has declined recently.

35 Connectors: Highlighting

Connectors are used to highlight examples.

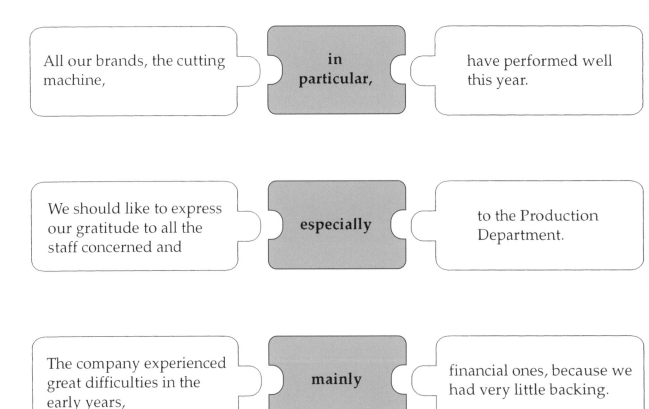

| All our brands, the cutting machine, | **in particular,** | have performed well this year. |

| We should like to express our gratitude to all the staff concerned and | **especially** | to the Production Department. |

| The company experienced great difficulties in the early years, | **mainly** | financial ones, because we had very little backing. |

We are planning to extend our operations in Asia, **chiefly** in Japan.

36 Reference words: Introduction

Reference words are used to:

- refer back to people, objects and ideas that have been mentioned earlier or
- refer forwards to people, objects and ideas that will be mentioned later.

These words allow the writer to avoid repeating words, paragraphs, and sometimes whole sentences.

Reference words include:

- it/they/them
- this/that
- these/those
- the former/the latter/respectively
- who/which/that
- one/ones
- such

Reference words: It/they/them

37

'It', 'they' and 'them' are used to replace subjects or ideas that have been mentioned previously.

(Relocating the factory to Bavaria) would seem to be sensible. **(It)** would save

the company a considerable amount of money each year.

(Bavaria) is an attractive region in which to live. **(It)** has mountains and lakes,

and is close to the ski resorts in Germany and Austria.

We have received a large number of (reports) about the economic outlook in Japan. We are studying (them) carefully. (They) contain useful marketing information.

Reference words: This/that/these/those

38

'**This**' and '**these**' are used to refer to objects or ideas that are near in place or time. For example, '**this**/**these** proposal(s)' mean(s) the one(s) just made or about to be made.

'**That**' and '**those**' are used to refer to objects or ideas that are more remote in place or time.

At our recent meeting, you suggested we (establish a joint venture in Russia).

(**This**) seems to be an attractive proposal, and I should like to discuss it with

you further.

Thank you for sending me some (samples of your products). (**These**) are

being inspected by our engineers, and we expect to make a purchase order in the

near future.

The Prime Minister was accused in the press of wishing to (increase taxation).

(**That**) is not the policy of the government, however, and the press reports are

incorrect.

Queries from (customers) are dealt with by the Customer Services Department.

(**Those**) who complain receive an answer within 24 hours.

39 Reference words: The former/the latter

When you have written about two subjects or two ideas, you may then wish to refer to them again in the next sentence. If you write 'it' or 'he', the reader may not understand which of the two you are referring to. You can use:

- **'the former'** which refers to the first mentioned of two items
- **'the latter'** which refers to the second mentioned of two items
- **'respectively'** which refers to each of the items in the order in which they were written, the former, then the latter

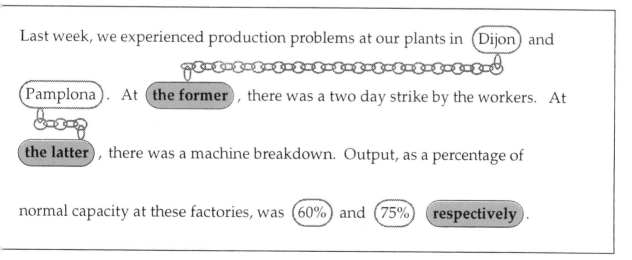

Last week, we experienced production problems at our plants in (Dijon) and (Pamplona). At (**the former**), there was a two day strike by the workers. At (**the latter**), there was a machine breakdown. Output, as a percentage of normal capacity at these factories, was (60%) and (75%) (**respectively**).

We will be visited on Tuesday 12 March by (Mr Laclos) and Mr Ibsen.

(**The former**) is the Managing Director of our operation in France and Italy.

Our new (6 Series) and (8 Series) models sell for (60,000 US dollars) and

(100,000 US dollars) (**respectively**) .

Reference words: Who/which/that

40

'**Who**' refers only to people. '**Which**' refers to things or ideas. '**That**' refers to people, things or ideas, and can be used instead of who or which.

Thank you for (your letter) of 25 October (**which**) I received today.

A dispute has arisen between management and the (sales staff) (**who**) think that

they are being asked to do too much.

At the conference, Mr Naumann will talk about the (developments) (that) are

taking place in the company.

'Which' can be used with 'all of', 'some of' or 'none of' to qualify the amount or number of the things being referred to:

The computers, **all of which** have been upgraded, will be in use from the beginning of next month.

The goods, **some of which** have been despatched already, should all have arrived by next Friday.

The prices, **none of which** has been changed, are listed in the brochure.

41 Reference words: One/ones

'**One**' (singular) or '**ones**' (plural) can be used as a substitute for a noun that has previously been mentioned.

There are two (relevant laws). The most important (**one**) refers to the rates of tax applicable.

I have quite a large number of 35 millimetre (slides) that you could borrow. I can let you have any of (**the ones**) I don't need myself.

There are (many problems to overcome), (**one of which**) is the security issue.

'**One of which**' can be used to refer to one item from a number of previously mentioned items.

There are (three new production assistants), (**one of whom**) is a French

graduate.

'**One of whom**' can be used to refer to one person from a number of previously mentioned people.

42 Reference words: Such

'**Such**' refers to things or people of a similar type to ones that have been mentioned previously.

Profits from selling investments are (capital gains). **Such** gains are taxable at a rate of 40%.

In recent months, we have experienced many (problems with the hardware). **Such** problems are not easy to solve and we have had to ask for technical assistance.

43 Referring to other parts of a text

When writing reports or complex letters and memos, it is often necessary to:

- refer back to an earlier part of the text
- refer forwards to something that is coming later
- refer to visuals such as graphs or statistical tables

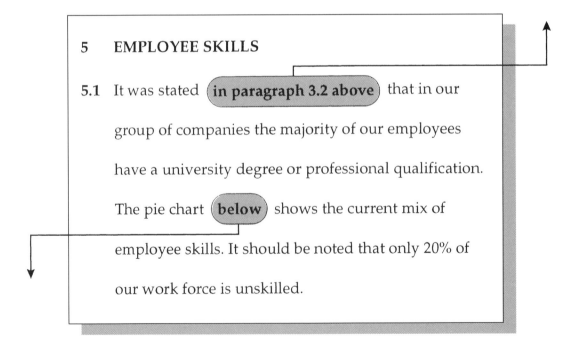

5   EMPLOYEE SKILLS

5.1 It was stated (**in paragraph 3.2 above**) that in our group of companies the majority of our employees have a university degree or professional qualification. The pie chart (**below**) shows the current mix of employee skills. It should be noted that only 20% of our work force is unskilled.

44 Referring to earlier parts of the text

We sometimes wish to refer back to something we wrote about earlier in a letter or report.

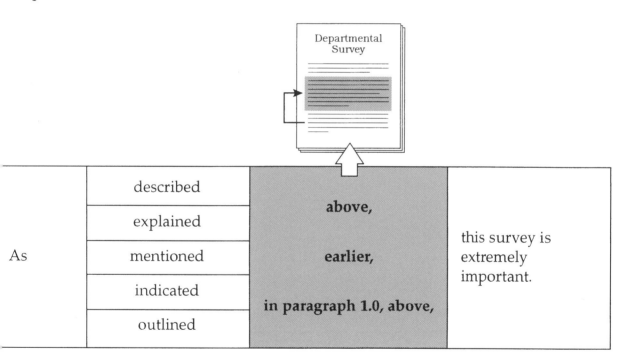

As				this survey is extremely important.
	described		**above,**	
	explained			
	mentioned		**earlier,**	
	indicated			
	outlined		**in paragraph 1.0, above,**	

| The | above | facts should be considered carefully. |
| | above-mentioned | |

| The facts | mentioned above | should be considered carefully. |

| Please see | Paragraph 1.2 | above. |

Referring forwards

45

We sometimes wish to indicate that we are going to write about something later in the letter or report.

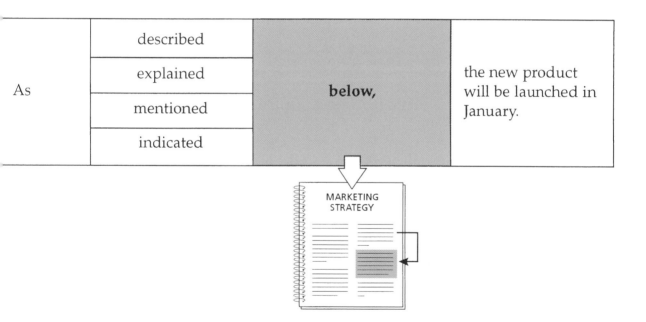

As	described	below,	the new product will be launched in January.
	explained		
	mentioned		
	indicated		

MARKETING STRATEGY

The following	procedure should be adhered to very carefully.

The procedure is	as follows:	1. survey carried out 2. report to the principal officer 3. necessary action taken.

46 Referring to visuals

We often wish to draw the reader's attention to a visual or a statistical table.

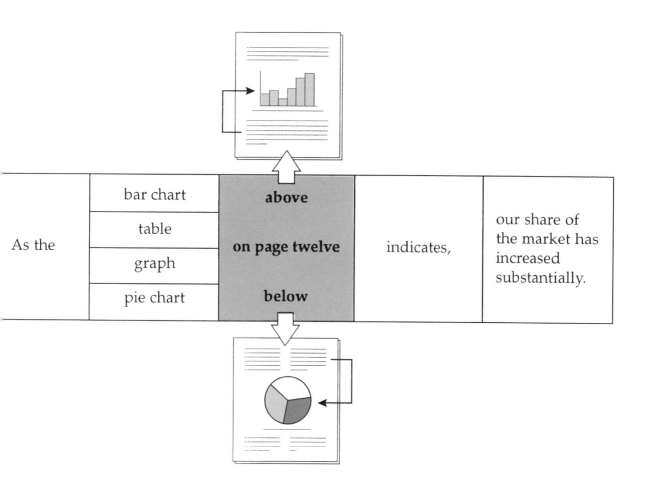

As the	bar chart	above	indicates,	our share of the market has increased substantially.
	table	**on page twelve**		
	graph			
	pie chart	below		

The table	**on page twelve** **above** **below**	shows gives	the relevant figures.

Please see	the graph	**on page 10.**

As indicated	in the	bar chart table graph pie chart	**below,** our largest markets are in South East Asia.

Clarity, Style and Tone

Introduction

47

Clarity

Clear writing is essential if your letters and reports are to be understood. In order to write clearly, you should first consider what it is that you wish to communicate to the reader and then write it clearly and simply.

Style

Style is the way you construct sentences to make writing more readable and therefore more understandable. It is important to use a variety of sentence constuctions and to choose the appropriate degree of formality.

Tone

Tone is the strength with which you express yourself in writing. Certain phrases are stronger than others. Choosing a strong, neutral or tentative phrase can significantly affect the message you give to the reader.

Clarity

48

There are a number of factors that affect how easy or difficult it is to read a text:

- the layout must be correct and attractive
- sentences should be short and simple in construction
- technical subject matter (jargon) should be kept to a minimum

Layout

There are many different layouts used for letters, reports and memos. These will be discussed later.

See Chapters 56-59.

Short sentences

If sentences are short and simple, text is easier to read and therefore easier to understand. Long sentences can be confusing because they will contain several statements or ideas. It is better, if possible, to use several shorter sentences.

Here are two ways of writing the same information. Version 1 shows the information as a single long sentence whereas it is shown as three shorter sentences in Version 2. Notice how Version 2 is easier to read and is clearer to understand.

Version 1

Whilst I accept your reasons for the delay in submitting your report on the advertising campaign, and notwithstanding the fact that the next meeting about advertising will not now be held until October, I must insist that you should complete it as quickly as possible, preferably before the end of the week, but no later than the beginning of September.

Version 2

I accept your reasons for the delay in submitting your report on the advertising campaign. Although the next advertising meeting will not now be held until October, I must insist that you should complete the report as quickly as possible. Please let me have it by the end of the week, or at least no later than the beginning of September.

Jargon

Technical subject matter

If you are writing to someone who is not an expert in your field of business, you should avoid using language that is too specialised or technical for the non-expert reader.

Here are two versions of the same extract from a report written by a banker in an investment bank. The meaning of Version 1 should be clear to other bankers, but might not mean anything to a person who does not understand banking terms. Version 2 avoids jargon and so is much clearer to read.

Version 1

The bank's position in US Treasuries is marked-to-market at the close of trade every day, and an unrealised profit or loss is reported.

Version 2

At the close of trade each day, the bank values its holdings of US Treasury bonds at current prices. A gain or loss is reported for the day, depending on whether the bond prices have moved favourably or unfavourably since the previous day.

Abbreviations

Avoid using abbreviations unless you are sure that the reader knows what they mean, otherwise the reader will be confused. Here is an example:

I have to submit a report on the CMQ to LAHQ by the end of the week. The DMSPR wants it urgently.

This may be clear if the reader is a colleague from the same organisation, but it may not be clear to someone outside the organisation!

49 Style

The style of a letter or report is affected by:

- the variety of sentence constructions
- the degree of formality used

Variety

Style can be improved by using a variety of sentence constructions. This makes the writing more interesting to read. The main topic of the sentence should appear at the beginning of the sentence to show that it is important.

The following examples show three ways of writing the same piece of information:

Because of the strike on the railways,	deliveries were unfortunately delayed by one week.

Here, the most important information is that the strike on the railways caused a problem.

Deliveries were delayed by one week	unfortunately because of the strike on the railways.

Here, the most important information is the problem that deliveries were delayed.

Unfortunately,	because of the strike on the railways, deliveries were delayed by one week.

Here, the most important information is the fact that something unfortunate occurred.

Here are two ways of writing the same text. Version 2 shows different forms of sentence construction and so is more interesting to read.

Version 1

I received your order for 10 desk fans on October 11. I regret to inform you that a labour strike has delayed production. We recently hired new staff. We expect to be back in production before the end of the month. I apologize for the delay.

Version 2

I received your order for 10 desk fans on October 11. Because of the labour strike in our factory, production on new desk fans has been delayed. Recently, we hired new staff and expect to be back in production before the end of the month. We sincerely apologize for the delay.

Formality

Written English is more formal than spoken language, especially in business letters and reports. The following points are important:

- contractions (we'll, it's, you've, etc.) are **not** normally used in business correspondence
- business letters and reports are more impersonal than letters to friends. 'We' is often used instead of 'I' when the writer represents a company
- the passive is often used as the reader is more interested in the action itself rather than who carried out the action

Formal and informal English

Here are some formal and informal phrases used in written English. Notice how most of the formal phrases use the passive.

INFORMAL	FORMAL
I recommend that you should close down the factory.	It is recommended/We recommend that you should close down the factory.
I have recently been told that...	It has recently come to my attention that...
We despatched the goods yesterday.	The goods were despatched yesterday.
Unless we act quickly, we shall lose this opportunity.	The opportunity will be lost unless we act quickly.
We purchase the components from Scandinavia.	The components are purchased from Scandinavia.

Both sets of phrases are correct, but should be used in different circumstances. For example, you might use an informal phrase when writing to a colleague you know wel whereas a formal phrase would be more appropriate when writing to another company

It is important to remember that, although written business English is more formal than spoken language, it is not as formal as it used to be. Some words and phrases that were previously used in letters are now considered to be over-formal. Here are some examples

OVER-FORMAL	BETTER
Our latest brochure is enclosed herewith.	We are pleased to enclose our latest brochure.
Pursuant to your enquiry, we...	Following your enquiry, we...

Spoken and written English

Here are some common words and phrases. Some are normally spoken, or are used for an informal writing style. An alternative word or phrase that might be used in a formal letter or report is shown in the next column.

SPOKEN

 WRITTEN

SPOKEN	WRITTEN
get worse	deteriorate
get better	improve
OK, alright	satisfactory
chance	opportunity
get in touch	contact
tell	inform
want	require
ask for	request
more information	further information
let me know if the date is alright	please confirm the date
fill in (a form)	complete (a form)
worried	concerned
guess	estimate
we are sorry	we regret
(to) help	(to) assist
help	assistance

Words and phrases in both columns may be used in spoken or written English, with the exception of 'OK' which is not used in business writing. In general, the words and phrases in the 'written' column are used when writing to someone outside your own company. It is also important not to use idiomatic language in formal letters and reports.

Tone

50

The tone with which you express yourself in writing can be:

- strong
- neutral
- tentative

For example, you may wish to express your view very strongly when making a recommendation in a letter or report.

Strong

You can use a strong tone to express an important view or recommendation. For example:

We strongly recommend that	you carry out a thorough review of your information systems.

We are firmly convinced that	the safety measures are inadequate.

If you are writing about legal requirements, you could use one of these phrases:

> It is obligatory that...
> You are legally required to...
> You are obliged by law to...

Neutral

You can use a neutral tone to suggest to the reader that your view or recommendation is worth considering, but is not a strong one. For example:

We recommend that	you carry out a thorough review of your information systems.

We believe that	the safety measures are inadequate.

Tentative

A tentative tone allows the reader to choose whether to act upon the view or to ignore it.

You might like to consider	carrying out a thorough review of your information systems.

It would seem that	the safety measures are inadequate.

Useful phrases

Here are some useful phrases, listed according to their strength:

STRONG	RECOMMENDATIONS	OPINIONS
	It is obligatory that...	We are firmly convinced that...
	You are legally required to...	We are firmly of the opinion that...
	It is of the utmost importance that...	
	We strongly recommend that...	

<table>
<tr><td rowspan="1" style="background:#ccc;">NEUTRAL</td><td colspan="2">RECOMMENDATIONS   OPINIONS</td></tr>
</table>

NEUTRAL		

RECOMMENDATIONS

We recommend that...

We advise you to...

It would be in your interest to...

You should consider...

OPINIONS

We believe that...

It is our opinion that...

TENTATIVE

RECOMMENDATIONS

You could consider...

You might like to consider...

OPINIONS

It would seem that...

It would appear that...

Structure

Introduction

When writing letters, reports and memos, it is important to:

- sequence your ideas
- write in short paragraphs
- link paragraphs in a logical sequence
- use headings and sub-headings
- use an appropriate layout

Sequencing ideas

52

Many business letters concern a situation or problem which has been analysed. In these cases, the writer may have considered one or more possible solutions or options. After this analysis, he or she may wish to make a recommendation to the reader. In this kind of letter or report, it is helpful to the reader if the following sequence is used:

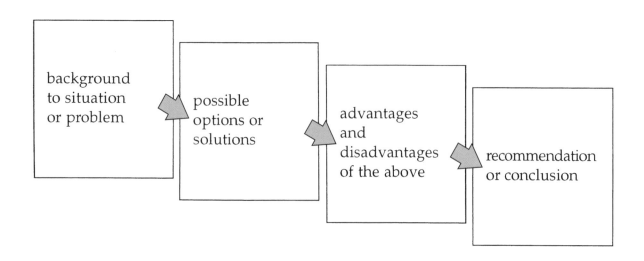

background to situation or problem → possible options or solutions → advantages and disadvantages of the above → recommendation or conclusion

WRITING SKILL

53 Paragraphs

Letters, reports and memos are clearer and easier to read if they are divided up into short paragraphs. A useful guideline is to have a separate paragraph for each idea or item.

Example

Here are two versions of the same extract from a report. Version 1 is not divided up, whereas Version 2 is divided into short paragraphs. Notice how much easier it is to read Version 2.

Version 1

The Internet, or World Wide Web as it is also called, is being promoted as the communications highway of the future. Our business has not been slow to recognise the potential benefits of this new medium for communication, especially now that material (text, sound or moving images) may be transmitted at high speed across the world. In addition, problems of security and unauthorised access to data are now being resolved at a technical level. An opportunity therefore exists, not only for software-based products (such as books, music and films) to be delivered over the Internet, but also a large range of financial services. Businesses can also take advantage of the Internet for the purpose of negotiating contracts and selling a large range of different products. If we do not look into the possibilities of using the Internet, our competitors might take the lead and gain an important advantage over us. Our position in the market would be seriously weakened. This report discusses the strategies that might be adopted by our company towards using the Internet to sell our products.

Version 2

The Internet, or World Wide Web as it is also called, is being promoted as the communications highway of the future.

Our business has not been slow to recognise the potential benefits of this new medium for communication, especially now that material (text, sound or moving images) may be transmitted at high speed across the world. In addition, problems of security and unauthorised access to data are now being resolved at a technical level.

An opportunity therefore exists, not only for software-based products (such as books, music and films) to be delivered over the Internet, but also a large range of financial services. Businesses can also take advantage of the Internet for the purpose of negotiating contracts and selling a large range of different products.

If we do not look into the possibilities of using the Internet, our competitors might take the lead and gain an important advantage over us. Our position in the market would be seriously weakened.

This report discusses the strategies that might be adopted by our company towards using the Internet to sell our products.

Paragraph linking

54

Although letters, reports and memos should be divided into paragraphs, there should be continuity. The ideas in one paragraph must lead to the ideas in the next paragraph. In other words, paragraphs must be linked with each other. Paragraph linking can be done in three ways:

- with connectors
- with reference words
- by using the same words in different paragraphs

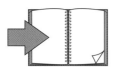

See the section on *Cohesion*.

Example

An example of paragraph linking is shown on the next page. The connector **'as a result'** is indicated by its shaded symbol; the other words which link the paragraphs are circled. For example, the word **'containers'** appears in the first and second paragraphs and **'delivery'/'deliveries'** in all three paragraphs.

As you know, there have been some problems with the (*delivery*) of (CONTAINERS) to Germany. It seems that (*delivery*) is 'frei Haus'. This means that the forwarding company is only obliged to (*deliver*) each consignment to the front door of the (*delivery*) address, which is an office block.

As a result, the (CONTAINERS) have been left at the entrance to the building, and have not been (*delivered*) to their destination on the fourth floor. Our own staff have had to carry the (CONTAINERS) from the entrance to the fourth floor.

Would it be possible in the future to arrange for (*deliveries*) to go 'frei Verwendungsstelle', which means to the place where the items are going to be used? We are prepared to pay a small extra charge for this service.

55 Headings and sub-headings

The clarity of letters, reports and memos is often improved by headings and sub-headings, which show what each section is all about.

Example

An extract from a company's handbook for employees, explaining the terms and conditions of employment, is shown on the next page. Notice how Version 2, with headings and sub-headings, helps the reader to see what is described in each paragraph.

Headings and sub-headings can be numbered in sequence, which makes it easier to read and follow a letter or report.

Version 1

Your monthly salary, less deduction, is paid to you by transfer to a bank account in your name. Your pay will be transferred to this account on or before the last working day of each month.

A payslip will be produced each month. It will show your salaries and allowances, the deductions made, and the net amount transferred to your bank account.

If you are sick, injured or unable to work for any other reason, you must notify your Manager, by telephone, as soon as possible on the first day of your absence.

You must provide a certificate from your doctor if you are absent for more that three days.

The company will pay your salary in full for the first four weeks of absence during a period of two years. If you are absent for a longer time than this, the company will reduce your salary to 50% of the normal amount.

Version 2

REMUNERATION

Your monthly salary, less deduction, is paid to you by transfer to a bank account in your name. Your pay will be transferred to this account on or before the last working day of each month.

A payslip will be produced each month. It will show your salaries and allowances, the deductions made, and the net amount transferred to your bank account.

SICKNESS AND ABSENCES

If you are sick, injured or unable to work for any other reason, you must notify your Manager, by telephone, as soon as possible on the first day of your absence.

Doctor's certificate
You must provide a certificate from your doctor if you are absent for more that three days.

Salary during absences
The company will pay your salary in full for the first four weeks of absence during a period of two years. If you are absent for a longer time than this, the company will reduce your salary to 50% of the normal amount.

56 Layout of business letters

Although there are many different layouts used for letters, they often follow the same general pattern:

- printed letterhead
- date
- reference
- addressee
- salutation
- main body
- closure
- a note about any enclosures or copies

An example of a typical British business letter is shown on the next page.

See Chapter 70, *Sample Letters*.

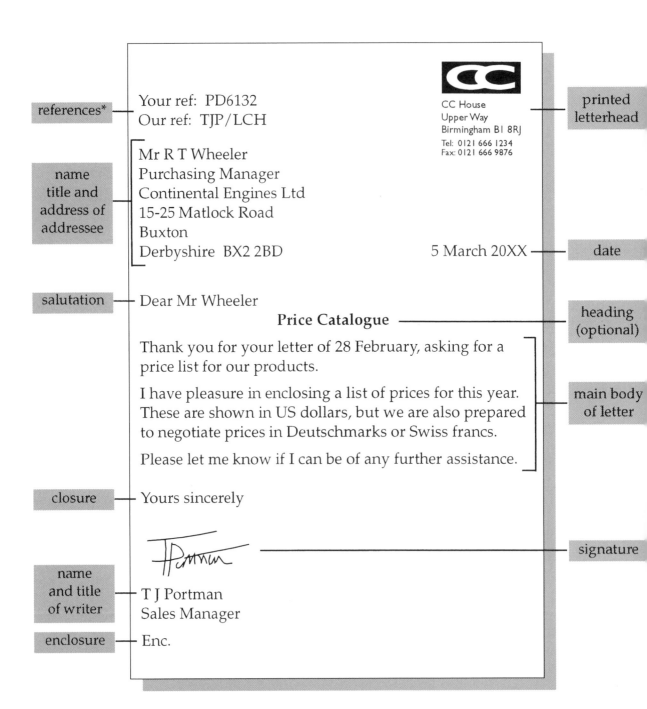

Your ref: PD6132
Our ref: TJP/LCH

CC

CC House
Upper Way
Birmingham B1 8RJ

Tel: 0121 666 1234
Fax: 0121 666 9876

printed
letterhead

name
title and
address of
addressee

Mr R T Wheeler
Purchasing Manager
Continental Engines Ltd
15-25 Matlock Road
Buxton
Derbyshire BX2 2BD

5 March 20XX

date

salutation

Dear Mr Wheeler

Price Catalogue

heading
(optional)

Thank you for your letter of 28 February, asking for a
price list for our products.

I have pleasure in enclosing a list of prices for this year.
These are shown in US dollars, but we are also prepared
to negotiate prices in Deutschmarks or Swiss francs.

Please let me know if I can be of any further assistance.

main body
of letter

closure

Yours sincerely

signature

name
and title
of writer

T J Portman
Sales Manager

enclosure

Enc.

* References are sometimes inserted here and sometimes above the salutation.

Date

	The date is usually positioned as shown in the example on the previous page but it is sometimes positioned above the salutation. It is normally written as:	1 March 20XX 11 June 20XX 23 August 20XX 30 November 20XX
	The date may be written as:	March 1, 20XX June 11, 20XX August 23, 20XX November 30, 20XX

!

In some British letters you may find the date written as follows, but this system is very rare now:

1st February, 20XX
13th June, 20XX
22nd October, 20XX
23rd December, 20XX

References

A reference is often used to refer to documents, purchase orders or manufacturers' orders. A reference can also be used to identify the writer of the letter, and the person who typed it. It is useful in future correspondence about the subject discussed in a letter. If you are replying to a letter, you should write the reference number cited in that letter, as well as your own reference.

Addressee

You should always write the name and address of the person to whom you are sending the letter.

Salutations and closures

Here is a list of some common salutations and closures.

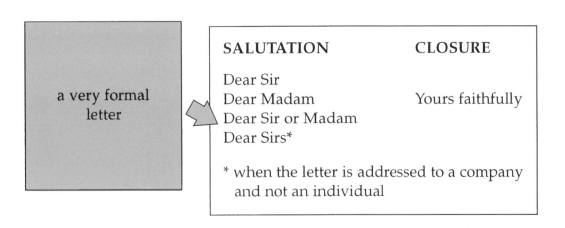

a very formal letter	SALUTATION	CLOSURE
	Dear Sir	
	Dear Madam	Yours faithfully
	Dear Sir or Madam	
	Dear Sirs*	
	* when the letter is addressed to a company and not an individual	

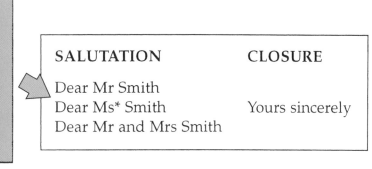

when you have met the person or have already exchanged letters or telephone calls	SALUTATION	CLOSURE
	Dear Mr Smith Dear Ms* Smith Dear Mr and Mrs Smith	Yours sincerely

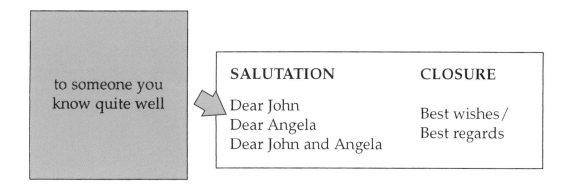

to someone you know quite well	SALUTATION	CLOSURE
	Dear John Dear Angela Dear John and Angela	Best wishes / Best regards

In British and American English, '**Ms**' can be used for both married and unmarried women and is now very common in written English.

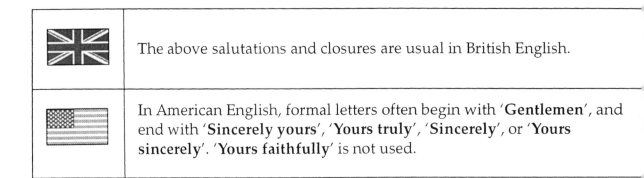

	The above salutations and closures are usual in British English.
	In American English, formal letters often begin with '**Gentlemen**', and end with '**Sincerely yours**', '**Yours truly**', '**Sincerely**', or '**Yours sincerely**'. '**Yours faithfully**' is not used.

Enclosures or copies

'**Enc.**', which is short for 'enclosure', is sometimes written at the bottom of a letter to indicate that another item is enclosed in the same envelope. An enclosure could be:

- a price list
- a brochure
- a catalogue
- a report
- a copy of an invoice

'**c.c.**' is used at the bottom of a letter to show that a copy of the letter is being sent to the person(s) named after the c.c. For example:

c.c.   T Hermann, Chief Executive
W. Kluwer, Sales Director

57 Layout of reports

Different companies may use different layouts for writing reports. The examples given in this chapter are standard formats. The structure of reports may vary according to the type of report.

There are two different types of report:

- those which give information (for example, a company report to shareholders)
- those which give the findings of research or investigations. These often contain a recommendation about a future course of action

Reports giving information

There is no standard structure for this type of report. It is, however, important to:

- group the information logically (there could be a chronological order or items could be ordered in terms of importance)
- divide the report into different sections with headings and sub-headings to make it easier for the reader to understand

Here is an extract from a Chairman's Report which gives information.

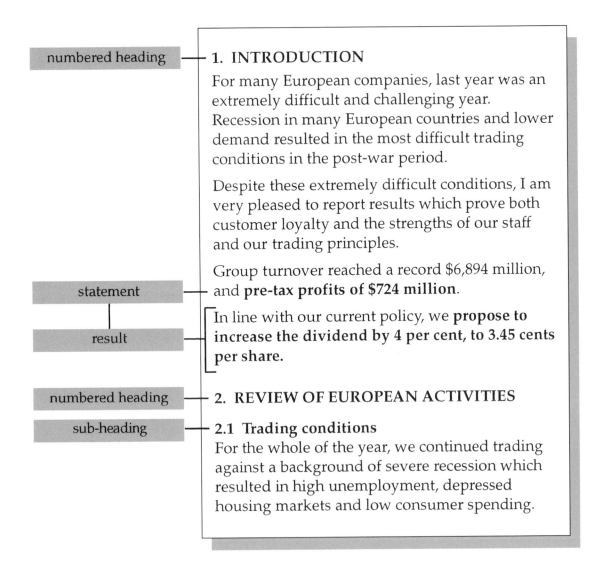

numbered heading → **1. INTRODUCTION**

For many European companies, last year was an extremely difficult and challenging year. Recession in many European countries and lower demand resulted in the most difficult trading conditions in the post-war period.

Despite these extremely difficult conditions, I am very pleased to report results which prove both customer loyalty and the strengths of our staff and our trading principles.

statement → Group turnover reached a record $6,894 million, and **pre-tax profits of $724 million**.

result → In line with our current policy, we **propose to increase the dividend by 4 per cent, to 3.45 cents per share.**

numbered heading → **2. REVIEW OF EUROPEAN ACTIVITIES**

sub-heading → **2.1 Trading conditions**
For the whole of the year, we continued trading against a background of severe recession which resulted in high unemployment, depressed housing markets and low consumer spending.

The expected boost in the economy in the second half of the year did not materialise and consumer confidence remained low. Nevertheless, we still managed to achieve positive results. Effective financial controls and some departmental restructuring speaks well of our management's ability to control the downside risk. In addition, it demonstrates the loyalty of our customers.

sub-heading — **2.2 Profitability**

Despite the growth of competitors, customers continued to appreciate the unique quality of our products. As a result of controlling costs while maintaining our high quality standards, the profitability of our European operators increased from 10.5% to 12.0% return on sales.

sub-heading — **2.3. Restructuring costs**

Restructuring in several departments and consequent redundancy payments have been taken as an exceptional cost against this year's profits.

3. CAPITAL EXPENDITURE

statements — **Group capital expenditure was higher than ever before at $260 million. 168 million dollars of this was spent on new retailing outlets and improvements to existing outlets. These costs**

explanation — **were met from retained earnings.**

Reports on research findings

Research reports normally follow this structure:

- title page
- contents list
- brief management summary
- introduction
- method of investigation, findings and recommendations
- conclusions
- references
- appendices

Title page

The title page will often contain:

- the title of the report
- the name of the company
- the name of the writer
- the date
- references

A report marked 'confidential' must only be read by the person to whom it is addressed, and the contents must be kept secret.

Here is an example of a title page:

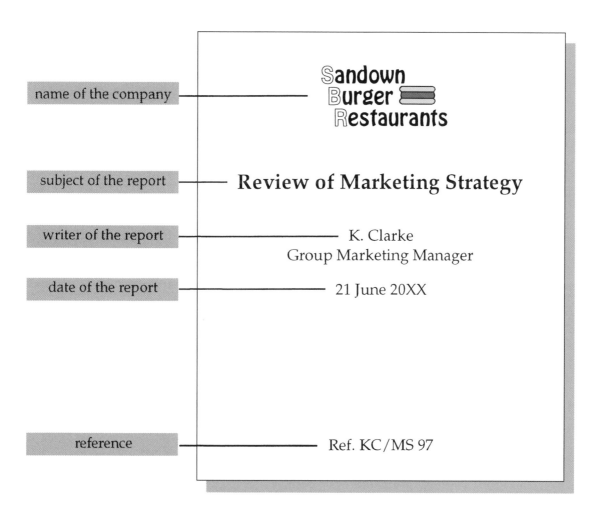

name of the company ——————— **Sandown Burger Restaurants**

subject of the report ——— **Review of Marketing Strategy**

writer of the report ——————— K. Clarke
Group Marketing Manager

date of the report ——————— 21 June 20XX

reference ——————— Ref. KC/MS 97

Contents list

The contents list should contain all the topics discussed in the report. For example:

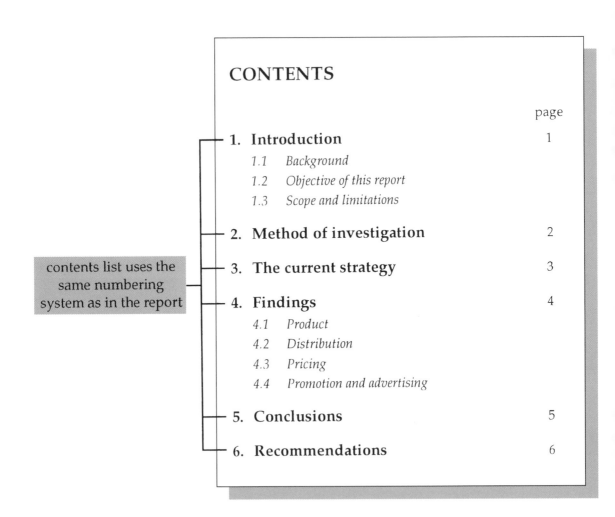

CONTENTS

page

1. **Introduction** 1
   - 1.1 *Background*
   - 1.2 *Objective of this report*
   - 1.3 *Scope and limitations*

2. **Method of investigation** 2

3. **The current strategy** 3

4. **Findings** 4
   - 4.1 *Product*
   - 4.2 *Distribution*
   - 4.3 *Pricing*
   - 4.4 *Promotion and advertising*

5. **Conclusions** 5

6. **Recommendations** 6

contents list uses the same numbering system as in the report

Brief management summary

This gives the reader a quick, concise summary of the report. It is usually less than one page long and does not contain any figures or data.

Introduction

The introduction explains:

- who has written the report, or what led up to the report (**background**)
- why the report has been written (**objective**)
- what the report covers, and what it does not cover (**scope** and **limitations**)

Here is an example:

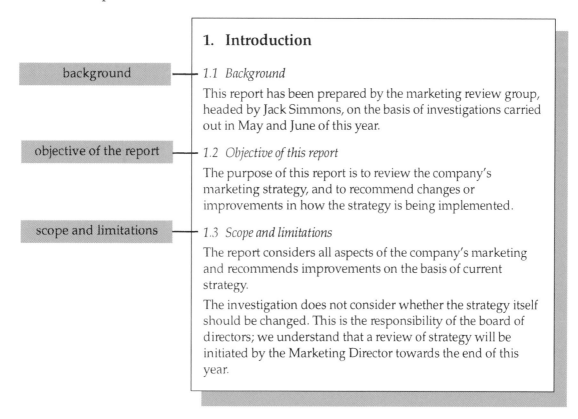

background

objective of the report

scope and limitations

1. Introduction

1.1 Background

This report has been prepared by the marketing review group, headed by Jack Simmons, on the basis of investigations carried out in May and June of this year.

1.2 Objective of this report

The purpose of this report is to review the company's marketing strategy, and to recommend changes or improvements in how the strategy is being implemented.

1.3 Scope and limitations

The report considers all aspects of the company's marketing and recommends improvements on the basis of current strategy.

The investigation does not consider whether the strategy itself should be changed. This is the responsibility of the board of directors; we understand that a review of strategy will be initiated by the Marketing Director towards the end of this year.

Methods, findings and recommendations

A report might explain:

- the methods of obtaining information used or presented in the report (**methods of investigation**)
- what the writer expected to find
- what the writer found (**findings**)
- any recommendations for actions to be taken

Here is an example of this section of a report. Notice how headings and sub-headings make the text easier to follow.

method of investigation or research

2. Methods of investigation

The marketing review group was divided into four teams, which looked at the product, distribution, pricing and promotion respectively.

The investigation was carried out over a four week period in May, by means of discussions with marketing managers at head office and restaurant managers at over fifty locations.

3. The current strategy

The marketing strategy of Sandown Limited for the past three years has been:

- to provide a range of good-quality meals to families, with an emphasis on 'healthy eating'
- to establish a solid market share at existing restaurant locations
- to maintain our image as a chain of reasonably-priced restaurants
- to change our image from fast-food restaurants to restaurants where families can enjoy a relaxed meal together

The strategy has been implemented by:

- the introduction of a new range of meals, using organically-grown vegetables and fruit
- improving the facilities at existing restaurants, with a $5 million expenditure programme
- reducing prices of main courses, but increasing prices of starter courses and drinks
- promoting the theme of relaxed family eating through television and billboard advertising

findings

4. Findings

Our investigations produced the following findings:

4.1 Product

Although new meals have been introduced to the menus in restaurants, only a few have been popular with customers. The rest have been sold in only small quantities, and restaurant managers would like to drop unsuccessful items from their menus. They claim that large quantities of unused food are thrown away each week.

4.2 Distribution

The $5 million expenditure programme has been completed. Restaurant managers have expressed their satisfaction with the improvements. Many customers praise the quality of the decor and facilities.

4.3 Pricing

Over the past three years the prices of main courses have been reduced on average by 20%. Prices of starters have been raised by 25% and drink prices have gone up by 10%. The effect on sales and profits appears to have varied between restaurants. On the whole, restaurants have increased both sales and profits during this time.

4.4 Promotion and advertising
An extensive advertising campaign is carried out each year. Market research suggests that the image of our restaurants as a place to have relaxed family meals has been recognised by the public.

The writer may include illustrations, such as charts, graphs or pictures, to support his or her discussion.

Conclusions

A report should end with conclusions or a summary of the findings. For example:

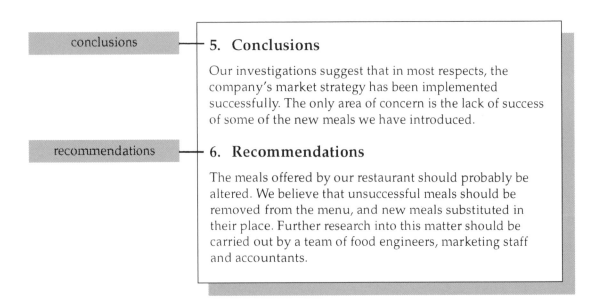

conclusions

5. Conclusions

Our investigations suggest that in most respects, the company's market strategy has been implemented successfully. The only area of concern is the lack of success of some of the new meals we have introduced.

recommendations

6. Recommendations

The meals offered by our restaurant should probably be altered. We believe that unsuccessful meals should be removed from the menu, and new meals substituted in their place. Further research into this matter should be carried out by a team of food engineers, marketing staff and accountants.

WRITING SKILL

References and appendices

At the end of a report there may be a **bibliography**, which is a list of all references or books used in writing the report. Entries in the bibliography should be alphabetised by the author's surname.

At the end of many reports is an **appendix**, which contains information that supports the findings of the report, such as charts, graphs or statistics.

	🇬🇧	🇺🇸
Singular	appendix	annex
Plural	appendices	annexes

Layout of memos

58

A memo is generally used as a way of communicating within a company. They give instructions and suggest actions that should be taken. Memos should be short, no longer that one or two pages.

Here is an example of a typical memo:

MEMORANDUM

To: Diana Trotter, Sales
From: Vicky Finch, Credit Control
Date: 27 February 20XX
Subject: Late payment by customers

An increasing number of our customers are failing to pay invoices on time. Sometimes payments are received up to six months late and delays are getting longer.

Our Department wishes to take action to speed up payments. Such measures might include refusing to give credit to some customers and insisting on payments with order.

Before any decisions are taken, however, I should appreciate the views of the Sales and Marketing Department on this matter.

Starting a memo

A memo should begin by stating:

- who the memo is being sent to (this can be more than one person)
- who the memo is being sent by
- the date
- a heading or title to indicate what the memo is about

Writing a memo

Here are some guidelines for writing a memo:

- keep it short
  use short sentences
- start the memo with an important statement or message
- write only what is necessary

Look at the following example. Version 1 is a letter from a company chairman to his marketing director. Version 2 is the same letter written in memo form.

Notice that the memo in Version 2:

- is shorter than the letter
  starts with an important message
- has short sentences

Version 1

17-23 Castle Street
Stafford
Staffs ST17 4DR
Tel: 01785 123 4567
Fax: 01785 765 4321

Peter Soper
Marketing Director
BDN Products Ltd   16 March 20XX

Dear Peter

As you know, I am giving a presentation to the European Engineering Conference in Madrid next week.

I thought the theme of my presentation should be **The Competition from Manufacturers in Asia**. This is a subject that concerns many companies in Europe.

To provide me with some background information for the presentation, I need to obtain some current data about the markets for engineering products.

Could you possibly let me have a copy of the market research report that your staff prepared last month? I think it might contain much of the data I need.

Regards

David Clifton
Chairman

Version 2

17-23 Castle Street
Stafford
Staffs ST17 4DR

Tel: 01785 123 4567
Fax: 01785 765 4321

MEMORANDUM

To: Peter Soper
From: David Clifton
Date: 16 March 20XX
Subject: Market Research Report

Could I please have a copy of your recent market research report? I need data about the engineering markets for my presentation in Madrid next month.

59 Fax and electronic mail

Fax* and electronic mail (or e-mail) are methods of sending letters, reports, memos and short messages.

* 'Fax' is the shortened form of 'facsimile'.

Fax messages

A fax message often has a cover page which contains the following information:

- the name and fax number of the person to whom the fax message is being sent
- the date
- the name of the writer
- the number of pages

A short message might be written or typed on this page.

A letter, report or memo sent by fax follows the cover page.

Here is an example of a typical fax message:

FAX MESSAGE

MSsLtd

To: Denise Plater
Fax number: 0263 41825
Date: 11 October 20XX
From: John Cross
Number of pages: 1 (including this page)

Denise,

I have looked at your report. I agree with what you say. Can you send a copy to Sandy Walker in Marketing?

Regards

E-mail

E-mail messages are sent from one computer to another. These do not have a standard layout. As a general rule, however, e-mail messages are short and are written in a style similar to memos.

Here is an example of an e-mail message.

FROM	Caroline Annis (28/8/XX)
TO	Jo-Anne Saxton
C.C.	Suzanne Coleman

Thanks for the report. I have passed on a copy to Frank's assistant, James.

Our next meeting with Frank is scheduled for Monday 19 September. Let me know if there's a problem with this date.

Can you make lunch tomorrow?

Punctuation

60 Introduction

The use of punctuation differs from one language to another. Punctuation conventions also change from time to time and modern letters and reports have, for example, fewer commas than in the past. Some punctuation rules, however, are more important than others.

This section of the book explains some of the more important rules for using punctuation in letters and reports.

Commas

61

When to use

Commas are used to separate items in a list:

> The main taxes in the
> UK are income tax
> corporation tax ,
> capital gains tax and
> Value Added Tax.

> Our main markets are
> in Sweden ,
> Denmark , Germany
> and Poland.

A comma is not used before the last item in a list when the last two items are joined by 'and'.

Commas are used after or in front of a word or phrase such as 'unfortunately' or 'in particular' which add something to a sentence:

Unfortunately (,) several of our sales team have left the company in recent weeks.

Finally (,) I should like to make the point that...

In 1996 (,) two new directors were appointed to the board.

Our brands performed extremely well in Scandanavia last year (,) in particular (,) in Sweden and Norway.

Commas are used before and after a non-defining relative clause (a clause which adds non-essential information):

The conference hotel (,) **which is very modern** (,) is in the centre of the city.

Commas are **not** used around defining relative clauses (clauses which give essential information), for example:

The ideas **discussed in the presentation** have given us a great deal to consider.

How use of commas can affect meaning

Use or non-use of commas can affect the meaning of a sentence. Look at the following examples:

Our customers **,** who have been invited to the trade fair **,** will be given a demonstration of the new model.	Our customers who have been invited to the trade fair will be given a demonstration of the new model.
All the customers have been invited to the trade fair and will be given a demonstration.	Not all of the customers have been invited to the trade fair and only those invited will be given a demonstration.

In English, unlike in some other languages, commas are not used in front of a 'that' or 'what' clause.

TYPICAL ERROR

The law states, that all companies must keep accounting records.

We complained, that the delivery was late.

They told us, what they planned to do.

CORRECT

The law **states that** all companies must keep accounting records.

We **complained that** the delivery was late.

They told **us what** they planned to do.

Colons

62

When to use

Colons are used to introduce a series or list of items:

The meeting has been
called to discuss the
following points :

1. this year's results
2. next year's budget
3. the appointment of a
    new director

The new office desks
are available in the
following colours :
grey, cream, beige and
black.

Colons are used to introduce a question or related statement following an independent clause:

Our main problem is transport : How do we get to the airport?

There is one explanation for our division's success : our excellent sales staff.

Semi-colons

63

When to use

Semi-colons are used to separate items in a long, complicated list which may already contain commas:

> The budget will be increased for the following areas of expenditure: personnel recruitment and training **;** production quality control, where a large investment in new machinery is required **;** sales and marketing, particularly in South America.

Semi-colons are used to separate clauses that are closely linked but that could be written as separate sentences:

Our competitors are doing extremely well (;) they are developing several new brands at the moment.

The invoices are on the desk (;) they need to be signed immediately.

We began by exporting our products to the Canadian market (;) we have since opened a factory in Philadelphia to produce goods in the US.

Apostrophes

When to use

Indicating possession

The apostrophe **goes before the s** ('s) for a singular item or person and for plural words that do not end in s (e.g. men, women, children, people). For example:

The company **'s** policy is to recruit university graduates.

one company

The sales people **'s** expenses must be kept under control.

lots of sales people

The apostrophe goes **after the s** (**s'**) for plural items or more than one person when the plural form ends in s:

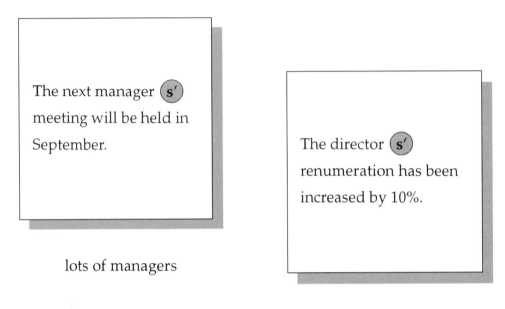

The next manager **s'** meeting will be held in September.

lots of managers

The director **s'** renumeration has been increased by 10%.

lots of directors

Replacing missing letters in contractions (shortened forms)

The apostrophe **replaces the missing letters** of the contracted (shortened) forms of auxiliary verbs. For example:

It **'s** a public company.

It **is** a public company.

We **'re** launching the new product next month.

We **are** launching the new product next month.

The delivery must **n't** be delayed.

The delivery **must not** be delayed.

Do not confuse **it's** (**it is**) with its (possessive pronoun which has no apostrophe). For example:

The company expanded **its** operations in Asia last year.

Shortened forms (**contractions**, e.g. don't, doesn't) are **not** used in formal written English. They are sometimes used in less formal memos and faxes, and in letters to friends, but not in business letters and reports.

65 Capital letters

Capital letters are used in English for the following:

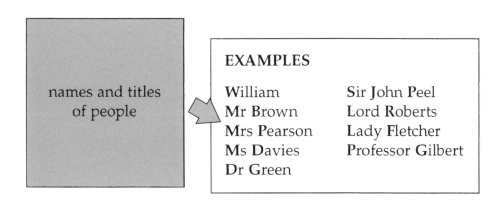

names and titles of people	**EXAMPLES**	
	William	Sir John Peel
	Mr Brown	Lord Roberts
	Mrs Pearson	Lady Fletcher
	Ms Davies	Professor Gilbert
	Dr Green	

official positions job titles official names	**EXAMPLES** Ministry of Finance President of the Board of Trade Inspector of Taxes Inland Revenue Department of Transport Lloyds Bank Jarvis Electronics Ltd **BMW AG**

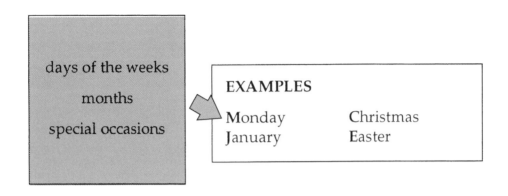

days of the weeks

months

special occasions

EXAMPLES

Monday   Christmas
January   Easter

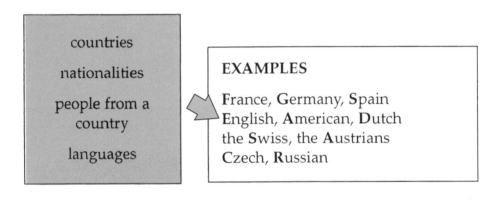

countries

nationalities

people from a
country

languages

EXAMPLES

France, Germany, Spain
English, American, Dutch
the Swiss, the Austrians
Czech, Russian

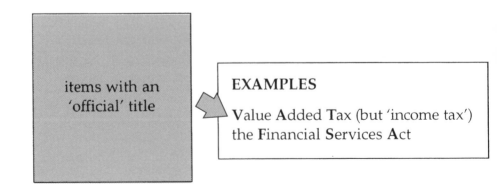

items with an
'official' title

EXAMPLES

Value Added Tax (but 'income tax')
the Financial Services Act

items that are identified by initials

EXAMPLES

RSVP (when you expect a response to a formal invitation)
R&D (research and development)
MBA (Master of Business Administration)
MD (Managing Director)

the first word of a sentence

EXAMPLE

The company was founded in 1980.

the personal pronoun 'I'

EXAMPLE

Finally, **I** recommend a review of the accounting system.

Capital letters are not used for other pronouns unless they are at the beginning of a sentence.

There are some exceptions to the rule about initial letters. Some initials can be written either all in capitals or all in small letters, for example:

plc/PLC = public limited company

British and
American Spellings

66 Some common differences

There are a few differences between British and American English spellings. Which type you use may depend on the convention in your company. The differences are small and it will not cause comprehension problems for readers whichever type you use. However, it is sensible to be consistent and to use either British or American spellings throughout your letter or report.

There has been a gradual tendency for some American spellings to be adopted in the UK. For example, '**program**' in 'computer program'. Also, the British now often use '..**ize**' in such words as '**organize**' – both endings are now acceptable in the UK.

Examples

BRITISH	AMERICAN
colour	color
labour	labor
programme	program
gramme	gram
centre	center
metre	meter
defence	defense
licence	license
practice (noun)	practice or practise
practise (verb)	practice
traveller	traveler
cancelled	canceled
generalise	generalize
organise	organize
naturalisation	naturalization

Common Problems

67 Introduction

Many non-native speakers from a variety of different countries often have similar problems in English. These may be problems with aspects of English grammar or with vocabulary. You may not experience all these problems yourself, but you will probably recognise some of them.

When you identify your own problems, you can use the checklists on pages 195-198. It can be very helpful to keep a list of your own common mistakes, together with a corrected version.

Grammar

68

When you are writing in English, it is very dangerous to try and translate word for word from your own language. Translating can cause problems with gramma for example:

- getting the word order wrong
- using the wrong prepositions
- using the wrong verb tense

This chapter will discuss some common grammatical problems.

Modal verbs

Modal verbs (e.g. **'can'**, **'must'**) are **never** followed by 'to'.

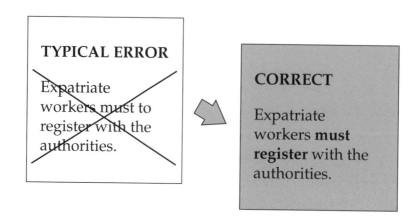

TYPICAL ERROR

Expatriate workers must to register with the authorities.

CORRECT

Expatriate workers **must register** with the authorities.

Auxiliary verbs (e.g. '**do**') are not used with modal verbs for questions and negatives. For example:

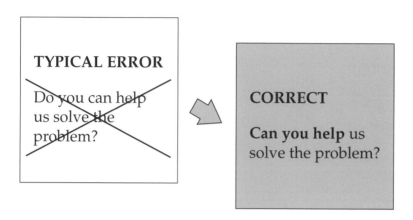

Adverbs and adjectives

Don't confuse adverbs with adjectives. Adverbs tell us more about verbs. Adjectives tell us more about nouns. Here are some typical errors to avoid.

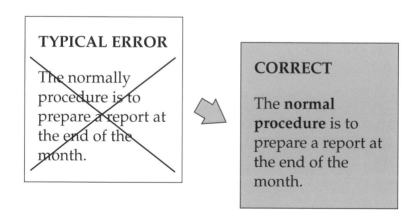

'Procedure' is a noun; requiring an adjective, 'normal'.

Adverbs can also be used to tell us more about adjectives. For example:

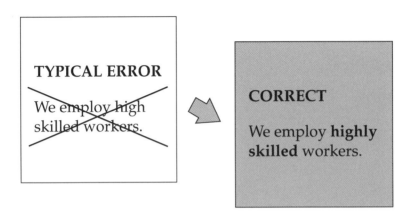

Word order

Verb/object

You should avoid putting adverbs or other words and phrases between the verb and the object. For example:

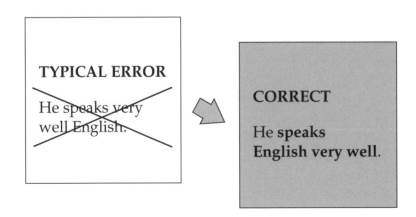

Verb/adverb

The adverb normally goes just before the main part of the verb. In negative sentences, 'probably' goes before the negative or before the modal or auxiliary verb. For example:

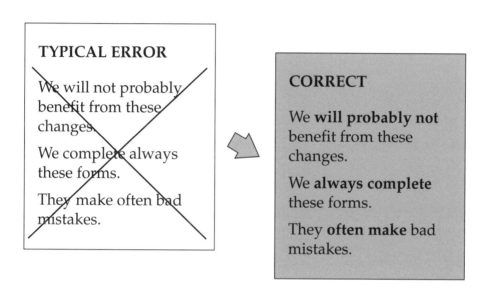

TYPICAL ERROR

We will not probably benefit from these changes.

We complete always these forms.

They make often bad mistakes.

CORRECT

We **will probably not** benefit from these changes.

We **always complete** these forms.

They **often make** bad mistakes.

Vocabulary

69

Words can be a problem when there is more than one with a similar meaning although these words may be used differently. Translating can also cause problems with vocabulary, for example, using words that exist in your own language which look similar to English words but which are not used in the same way. This chapter will look at some examples of common vocabulary problems.

For, since and ago

'**For**' is used with a period of time or a number of days, weeks, months, years. For example:

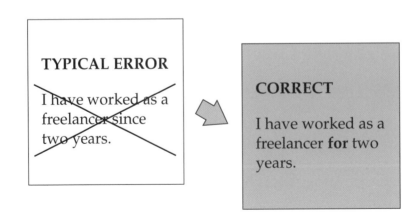

TYPICAL ERROR

~~I have worked as a freelancer since two years.~~

CORRECT

I have worked as a freelancer **for** two years.

'**Since**' is used with a point in time, for example, January, January 1, Sunday, 1990.

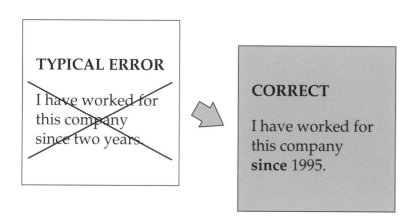

'**Ago**' is used to say when something happened in the past, by counting backwards from the present, for example, 'four years ago'.

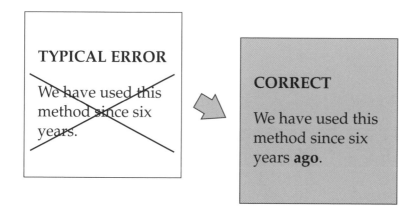

In case and if

'**In case**' does not mean the same as '**if**'. **In case** is used to talk about precautions taken in advance to avoid potential difficulties. **If** is used in conditional sentences.

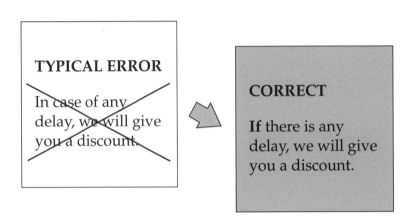

When and if

'**When**' is used when something is certain to happen. '**If**' is used when we are unsure whether something will happen or not.

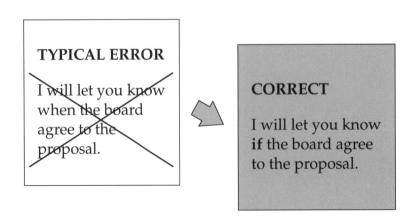

WRITING SKILL

Do and make

Do' and 'make' are often confused because in many other languages, there is only one verb, rather than the two which exist in English.

Do' is used to talk about an activity when we do not say exactly what it is:

We plan to **do** it next summer.

I don't know what to **do** about this problem.

Do' is used when we talk about work:

I have an important job for you to **do**.

We have **done** a great deal of work on this project.

'**Do**' is used with words like 'good', 'harm', 'business', 'one's best' and 'a favour':

We have been **doing** business in Belgium for ten years.

We will **do** our best to complete the order on time.

'**Make**' often expresses the idea of creation or construction. It is used with the following:

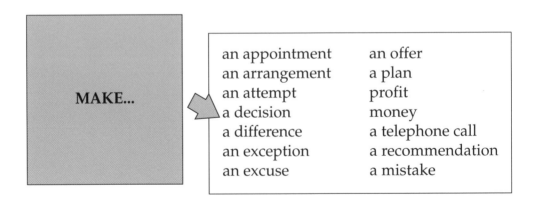

MAKE...

an appointment	an offer
an arrangement	a plan
an attempt	profit
a decision	money
a difference	a telephone call
an exception	a recommendation
an excuse	a mistake

False friends

'**False friends**' are words that exist in your own language and look similar to English words, but which are not used in the same way. Here are some common 'false friends':

● '**Actual**' means **real**, not 'present'

> **Actual** profits last month were below budget.

● '**Eventually**' means **finally**, not 'possibly'

> After a lot of research, we **eventually** found the information we needed.

- '**Control**' means to supervise or have authority over something. It does not mean 'check'. '**Check**' means to look at something to see if it is correct.

> Costs must be rigorously **controlled** to ensure that they do not rise too fast.

> The auditors are **checking** the accounts at the moment.

- '**Become**' means **come to be**, it does not mean 'get' or 'receive'. When talking about receiving a letter, for example, you can use '**get**' or '**receive**'.

> He worked as a clerk in the sales department ten years ago, and last year, he **became** the Sales Manager.

> I **received** a letter from the suppliers this morning.

Personal Checklist

Use this checklist to note examples of mistakes you often make, together with the correct version.

MISTAKES I OFTEN MAKE	CORRECT

MISTAKES I OFTEN MAKE	CORRECT

MISTAKES I OFTEN MAKE	CORRECT

MISTAKES I OFTEN MAKE	CORRECT

Sample
Business Letters

Sample letters

70

This chapter contains a number of different types of business letter:

- an enquiry
- a response to an enquiry
- asking for a price quotation
- giving a price quotation
- placing an order
- a complaint
- asking for an overdue payment

If you wish, you can use these letters as an outline for similar letters that you might write in the future.

An enquiry

FibrOptics Ltd
Landsend Road
Leatherhead
Surrey
KT22 4HP

Tel 01372 455454
Fax 01372 680246

The Sales Director
Technix Trading Ltd
58 Rugby Road
Birmingham
B12 8VB

22 October 20XX

Dear Sir

I understand that you are a distributor of underwater cameras.

We are planning to purchase up to 10 such cameras in the next few months, and are trying to find out what products are available on the market.

Would you please send me details of the cameras you supply, with prices.

Yours faithfully

M Gibson

Michael Gibson
Operations Manager

This letter is written to a distributor of a product. A similar letter could be sent to a manufacturer or supplier of a product.

The writer asks for details about the products, and prices. An enquiry could also ask for a catalogue, a brochure or samples of the product.

Response to an enquiry

Michael Gibson
Operations Manager
Fibroptics Ltd
Landsend Road
Leatherhead
Surrey
KT22 4HP

Technix
Trading

58 Rugby Road
Birmingham
B12 5VB
Tel 0121 212 8788
Fax 0121 212 6040

28 October 20XX

Dear Mr Gibson

Thank you for your enquiry of 22 October.

I enclose a catalogue and price list for our cameras.

Our sales representative for the South of England, John Poole, would be pleased to visit you to give a demonstration. His telephone number is 0208 625 4183.

We can usually deliver within 2 to 3 weeks of receiving an order. Payment terms are 30 days net.

If you need any further information, please let me know.

Yours sincerely

Monica Bridges

Monica Bridges
Sales Director

Another opening sentence to this letter could be '**Thank you for your letter of 22 October**' or '**With reference to your letter of 22 October**'.

If the writer wanted to be more polite, she could have written '**I have pleasure in enclosing a catalogue and price list...**'.

Asking for a price quotation

Cordex Chemicals plc

Pinafore House
50 Gateshead Road
Newcastle upon Tyne
NE17 7LZ
Tel 0191 206 1317
Fax 0191 206 4065

Mr D W Warner
Tightline Printing Ltd
218 Naylor Street
Gateshead
NE28 4QQ

8 December 20XX

Dear Mr Warner

Further to our telephone conversation today, I should like to confirm our printing specifications.

Item	Company Report
Quantity	10,000 - 20,000 copies
Paper quality	120gsm, coated
Cover	160gsm, laminated
Page size	A4
Number of pages	32
Colour	4 colour

Could you please quote a price for this work, and indicate your terms of payment.

Yours sincerely

Vincent O'Reilly
Company Secretary

Giving a price quotation

Tightline Printing Ltd

218 Naylor Street
Gateshead
NE28 4QQ
Tel 0191 384 1612

Cordex Chemicals plc
Pinafore House
50 Gateshead Road
Newcastle upon Tyne
NE17 7LZ

12 December 20XX

Dear Mr O'Reilly

In reply to your enquiry of 8 December, I have pleasure in submitting the following price quotation:

10,000 copies	£40,000
For each additional 1,000 copies	£2,000

This price includes the cost of delivery to a single destination in the UK.

Payment terms are 30 days net.

I look forward to hearing from you, and assure you that your order will receive our immediate attention.

Yours sincerely

D W Warner

This reply is fairly formal and polite. This is evident in the use of the expressions **'I have pleasure in...'** and **'I look forward to...'** and **'assure you that...'**.

The payment terms state the arrangements that would be expected for payment by the customer. **'30 days net'** means that the invoice should be paid in full within 30 days of the date of the invoice.

Placing an order

Commercial Software Ltd

Raglan House
108 McDonald Street
Glasgow
G3 2ST

Telephone 0141 826 7153
Fax 0141 826 7284

DX Office Suppliers Ltd
8 Queen Street
Glasgow
G2 4JD

31 July 20XX

Dear Sir

I wish to order the following items from your catalogue:

Quantity	Item	Catalogue Number
12	Desks	F1863327
12	Swivel chairs	F2710039
18	Filing cabinets	F2308452

I understand that you can arrange delivery of these items within one week.

Please send the invoice for my attention.

Yours faithfully

P A Eales
Director

Trans Panels Ltd

Northern Works
East Bristol Industrial Estate
Bristol
BS4 7RA

Telephone 0117 780100
Fax 0117 784935

Ms R E Taverner
Electra Maintenance Engineering Ltd
EME House
40 Bath Road
Bristol
BS6 3BA

22 January 20XX

Dear Ms Taverner

Thank you for your letter of 2 June, in which you quoted a price for a maintenance contract for our robotic equipment.

We are pleased to inform you that we wish to accept your offer at the quoted price and on the specified terms.

Could you please telephone me in the next few days, to discuss arrangements for signing the contract.

Yours sincerely

Tom Gardiner
Production Director

Letter of complaint: Late delivery

Rhone Clothing Ltd

8 Bedford Square
London
W1A 7CT

Tel 0207 630 8000
Fax 0207 834 2153

B A King
Eastern Textiles Ltd
38 The Hill
Brighton
BN2 6XZ

11 November 20XX

Dear Mr King

Order number RC 632119 of 15 April 20XX

The goods we ordered from you in April this year were delivered to our warehouse yesterday.

When we placed the order, we specified that delivery must take place by the end of September at the latest. A large proportion of our annual sales occurs during September and October. As a result of your late delivery, we do not expect to find customers for the items you have supplied.

I regret that I must ask you to take back the goods from our warehouse, at your own expense. I must also insist that in any future arrangements, you must observe the deadline for delivery that we specify in our purchase order.

Yours sincerely

Don Madden
Chief Buyer

Letter of complaint: Poor quality goods

Gamma Oil plc

Gamma House
Manchester
M1 1AB

Tel 0161 232 3000
Fax 0161 385 5676

AD Trading Ltd
Solomon House
2 Bedford Square
London
W1A 3PP

29 June 20XX

Dear Sir

We recently purchased a quantity of oil from you, which was delivered to Dar-es-Salaam this week.

On inspection, we have found that the oil does not meet the specifications in our purchase agreement and is of an inferior quality.

We do not wish to accept a consignment of sub-standard quality, and we have instructed our office in Dar-es-Salaam accordingly.

Yours faithfully

P A S Lowther
Operations Director

Asking for an overdue payment

Woodburn Systems Ltd

Gamma House
Manchester
M1 1AB

Tel 0161 232 3000
Fax 0161 385 5676

Our Ref: Invoice 3187825

Accounts Department
Frampton Hydraulics Ltd
Unit 10
Livermore Industrial Estate
Bromley Kent
BR3 4TP

17 May 20XX

Dear Sir

OVERDUE PAYMENT

We are surprised that invoice 3187825, dated 3 March, is overdue for payment.

May we remind you that our terms of payment are strictly one month after the invoice date. Payment was therefore due on 3 April.

Should there be some difficulty in meeting our payment terms or if there is any query about the invoice, please contact this department immediately.

We look forward, however, to your prompt settlement and trust that no further action on our part will be necessary.

Yours faithfully

T R Munton
Supervisor, Accounts Department